C-3867   CAREER EXAMINATION SERIES

This is your
PASSBOOK for...

Watch, Guard and Patrol License

Test Preparation Study Guide
Questions & Answers

COPYRIGHT NOTICE

This book is SOLELY intended for, is sold ONLY to, and its use is RESTRICTED to individual, bona fide applicants or candidates who qualify by virtue of having seriously filed applications for appropriate license, certificate, professional and/or promotional advancement, higher school matriculation, scholarship, or other legitimate requirements of education and/or governmental authorities.

This book is NOT intended for use, class instruction, tutoring, training, duplication, copying, reprinting, excerption, or adaptation, etc., by:

1) Other publishers
2) Proprietors and/or Instructors of "Coaching" and/or Preparatory Courses
3) Personnel and/or Training Divisions of commercial, industrial, and governmental organizations
4) Schools, colleges, or universities and/or their departments and staffs, including teachers and other personnel
5) Testing Agencies or Bureaus
6) Study groups which seek by the purchase of a single volume to copy and/or duplicate and/or adapt this material for use by the group as a whole without having purchased individual volumes for each of the members of the group
7) Et al.

Such persons would be in violation of appropriate Federal and State statutes.

PROVISION OF LICENSING AGREEMENTS – Recognized educational, commercial, industrial, and governmental institutions and organizations, and others legitimately engaged in educational pursuits, including training, testing, and measurement activities, may address request for a licensing agreement to the copyright owners, who will determine whether, and under what conditions, including fees and charges, the materials in this book may be used them. In other words, a licensing facility exists for the legitimate use of the material in this book on other than an individual basis. However, it is asseverated and affirmed here that the material in this book CANNOT be used without the receipt of the express permission of such a licensing agreement from the Publishers. Inquiries re licensing should be addressed to the company, attention rights and permissions department.

All rights reserved, including the right of reproduction in whole or in part, in any form or by any means, electronic or mechanical, including photocopying, recording, or by any information storage and retrieval system, without permission in writing from the Publisher.

Copyright © 2024 by
National Learning Corporation

212 Michael Drive, Syosset, NY 11791
(516) 921-8888 • www.passbooks.com
E-mail: info@passbooks.com

PUBLISHED IN THE UNITED STATES OF AMERICA

PASSBOOK® SERIES

THE *PASSBOOK® SERIES* has been created to prepare applicants and candidates for the ultimate academic battlefield – the examination room.

At some time in our lives, each and every one of us may be required to take an examination – for validation, matriculation, admission, qualification, registration, certification, or licensure.

Based on the assumption that every applicant or candidate has met the basic formal educational standards, has taken the required number of courses, and read the necessary texts, the *PASSBOOK® SERIES* furnishes the one special preparation which may assure passing with confidence, instead of failing with insecurity. Examination questions – together with answers – are furnished as the basic vehicle for study so that the mysteries of the examination and its compounding difficulties may be eliminated or diminished by a sure method.

This book is meant to help you pass your examination provided that you qualify and are serious in your objective.

The entire field is reviewed through the huge store of content information which is succinctly presented through a provocative and challenging approach – the question-and-answer method.

A climate of success is established by furnishing the correct answers at the end of each test.

You soon learn to recognize types of questions, forms of questions, and patterns of questioning. You may even begin to anticipate expected outcomes.

You perceive that many questions are repeated or adapted so that you can gain acute insights, which may enable you to score many sure points.

You learn how to confront new questions, or types of questions, and to attack them confidently and work out the correct answers.

You note objectives and emphases, and recognize pitfalls and dangers, so that you may make positive educational adjustments.

Moreover, you are kept fully informed in relation to new concepts, methods, practices, and directions in the field.

You discover that you are actually taking the examination all the time: you are preparing for the examination by "taking" an examination, not by reading extraneous and/or supererogatory textbooks.

In short, this PASSBOOK®, used directedly, should be an important factor in helping you to pass your test.

WATCH, GUARD AND PATROL LICENSE

DUTIES
Under supervision, performs routine work consisting of minor tasks of a varied nature necessary for the patrolling, inspecting, and watching of public buildings and grounds to protect against, or prevent trespassing, prowling, damage to and loss of city property; performs related work.

EXAMPLES OF TYPICAL TASKS
Under supervision, and with no power of arrest or summons, patrols and makes periodic inspection tours of buildings, grounds, and assigned facilities to examine gates, windows, doors, locks, and equipment; watches for trespassers, prowlers, fires, or any other incident which may result in loss of or damage to city property; discourages loitering and misuse of equipment or facilities; maintains order and, when on a day shift, may assist a human resources administration special officer with the detention or handling of disorderly persons in assigned areas.

SCOPE OF THE WRITTEN TEST
The written test will be of the multiple-choice type and may include questions on judgment in job situations; understanding simple instructions and using simple vocabulary; preparing and comprehending simple written material.

HOW TO TAKE A TEST

I. YOU MUST PASS AN EXAMINATION

A. *WHAT EVERY CANDIDATE SHOULD KNOW*

Examination applicants often ask us for help in preparing for the written test. What can I study in advance? What kinds of questions will be asked? How will the test be given? How will the papers be graded?

As an applicant for a civil service examination, you may be wondering about some of these things. Our purpose here is to suggest effective methods of advance study and to describe civil service examinations.

Your chances for success on this examination can be increased if you know how to prepare. Those "pre-examination jitters" can be reduced if you know what to expect. You can even experience an adventure in good citizenship if you know why civil service exams are given.

B. *WHY ARE CIVIL SERVICE EXAMINATIONS GIVEN?*

Civil service examinations are important to you in two ways. As a citizen, you want public jobs filled by employees who know how to do their work. As a job seeker, you want a fair chance to compete for that job on an equal footing with other candidates. The best-known means of accomplishing this two-fold goal is the competitive examination.

Exams are widely publicized throughout the nation. They may be administered for jobs in federal, state, city, municipal, town or village governments or agencies.

Any citizen may apply, with some limitations, such as the age or residence of applicants. Your experience and education may be reviewed to see whether you meet the requirements for the particular examination. When these requirements exist, they are reasonable and applied consistently to all applicants. Thus, a competitive examination may cause you some uneasiness now, but it is your privilege and safeguard.

C. *HOW ARE CIVIL SERVICE EXAMS DEVELOPED?*

Examinations are carefully written by trained technicians who are specialists in the field known as "psychological measurement," in consultation with recognized authorities in the field of work that the test will cover. These experts recommend the subject matter areas or skills to be tested; only those knowledges or skills important to your success on the job are included. The most reliable books and source materials available are used as references. Together, the experts and technicians judge the difficulty level of the questions.

Test technicians know how to phrase questions so that the problem is clearly stated. Their ethics do not permit "trick" or "catch" questions. Questions may have been tried out on sample groups, or subjected to statistical analysis, to determine their usefulness.

Written tests are often used in combination with performance tests, ratings of training and experience, and oral interviews. All of these measures combine to form the best-known means of finding the right person for the right job.

II. HOW TO PASS THE WRITTEN TEST

A. NATURE OF THE EXAMINATION

To prepare intelligently for civil service examinations, you should know how they differ from school examinations you have taken. In school you were assigned certain definite pages to read or subjects to cover. The examination questions were quite detailed and usually emphasized memory. Civil service exams, on the other hand, try to discover your present ability to perform the duties of a position, plus your potentiality to learn these duties. In other words, a civil service exam attempts to predict how successful you will be. Questions cover such a broad area that they cannot be as minute and detailed as school exam questions.

In the public service similar kinds of work, or positions, are grouped together in one "class." This process is known as *position-classification*. All the positions in a class are paid according to the salary range for that class. One class title covers all of these positions, and they are all tested by the same examination.

B. FOUR BASIC STEPS

1) Study the announcement

How, then, can you know what subjects to study? Our best answer is: "Learn as much as possible about the class of positions for which you've applied." The exam will test the knowledge, skills and abilities needed to do the work.

Your most valuable source of information about the position you want is the official exam announcement. This announcement lists the training and experience qualifications. Check these standards and apply only if you come reasonably close to meeting them.

The brief description of the position in the examination announcement offers some clues to the subjects which will be tested. Think about the job itself. Review the duties in your mind. Can you perform them, or are there some in which you are rusty? Fill in the blank spots in your preparation.

Many jurisdictions preview the written test in the exam announcement by including a section called "Knowledge and Abilities Required," "Scope of the Examination," or some similar heading. Here you will find out specifically what fields will be tested.

2) Review your own background

Once you learn in general what the position is all about, and what you need to know to do the work, ask yourself which subjects you already know fairly well and which need improvement. You may wonder whether to concentrate on improving your strong areas or on building some background in your fields of weakness. When the announcement has specified "some knowledge" or "considerable knowledge," or has used adjectives like "beginning principles of..." or "advanced ... methods," you can get a clue as to the number and difficulty of questions to be asked in any given field. More questions, and hence broader coverage, would be included for those subjects which are more important in the work. Now weigh your strengths and weaknesses against the job requirements and prepare accordingly.

3) Determine the level of the position

Another way to tell how intensively you should prepare is to understand the level of the job for which you are applying. Is it the entering level? In other words, is this the position in which beginners in a field of work are hired? Or is it an intermediate or advanced level? Sometimes this is indicated by such words as "Junior" or "Senior" in the class title. Other jurisdictions use Roman numerals to designate the level – Clerk I, Clerk II, for example. The word "Supervisor" sometimes appears in the title. If the level is not indicated by the title, check the description of duties. Will you be working under very close supervision, or will you have responsibility for independent decisions in this work?

4) Choose appropriate study materials

Now that you know the subjects to be examined and the relative amount of each subject to be covered, you can choose suitable study materials. For beginning level jobs, or even advanced ones, if you have a pronounced weakness in some aspect of your training, read a modern, standard textbook in that field. Be sure it is up to date and has general coverage. Such books are normally available at your library, and the librarian will be glad to help you locate one. For entry-level positions, questions of appropriate difficulty are chosen – neither highly advanced questions, nor those too simple. Such questions require careful thought but not advanced training.

If the position for which you are applying is technical or advanced, you will read more advanced, specialized material. If you are already familiar with the basic principles of your field, elementary textbooks would waste your time. Concentrate on advanced textbooks and technical periodicals. Think through the concepts and review difficult problems in your field.

These are all general sources. You can get more ideas on your own initiative, following these leads. For example, training manuals and publications of the government agency which employs workers in your field can be useful, particularly for technical and professional positions. A letter or visit to the government department involved may result in more specific study suggestions, and certainly will provide you with a more definite idea of the exact nature of the position you are seeking.

III. KINDS OF TESTS

Tests are used for purposes other than measuring knowledge and ability to perform specified duties. For some positions, it is equally important to test ability to make adjustments to new situations or to profit from training. In others, basic mental abilities not dependent on information are essential. Questions which test these things may not appear as pertinent to the duties of the position as those which test for knowledge and information. Yet they are often highly important parts of a fair examination. For very general questions, it is almost impossible to help you direct your study efforts. What we can do is to point out some of the more common of these general abilities needed in public service positions and describe some typical questions.

1) General information

Broad, general information has been found useful for predicting job success in some kinds of work. This is tested in a variety of ways, from vocabulary lists to questions about current events. Basic background in some field of work, such as sociology or economics, may be sampled in a group of questions. Often these are principles which have become familiar to most persons through exposure rather than through formal training. It is difficult to advise you how to study for these questions; being alert to the world around you is our best suggestion.

2) Verbal ability

An example of an ability needed in many positions is verbal or language ability. Verbal ability is, in brief, the ability to use and understand words. Vocabulary and grammar tests are typical measures of this ability. Reading comprehension or paragraph interpretation questions are common in many kinds of civil service tests. You are given a paragraph of written material and asked to find its central meaning.

3) Numerical ability

Number skills can be tested by the familiar arithmetic problem, by checking paired lists of numbers to see which are alike and which are different, or by interpreting charts and graphs. In the latter test, a graph may be printed in the test booklet which you are asked to use as the basis for answering questions.

4) Observation

A popular test for law-enforcement positions is the observation test. A picture is shown to you for several minutes, then taken away. Questions about the picture test your ability to observe both details and larger elements.

5) Following directions

In many positions in the public service, the employee must be able to carry out written instructions dependably and accurately. You may be given a chart with several columns, each column listing a variety of information. The questions require you to carry out directions involving the information given in the chart.

6) Skills and aptitudes

Performance tests effectively measure some manual skills and aptitudes. When the skill is one in which you are trained, such as typing or shorthand, you can practice. These tests are often very much like those given in business school or high school courses. For many of the other skills and aptitudes, however, no short-time preparation can be made. Skills and abilities natural to you or that you have developed throughout your lifetime are being tested.

Many of the general questions just described provide all the data needed to answer the questions and ask you to use your reasoning ability to find the answers. Your best preparation for these tests, as well as for tests of facts and ideas, is to be at your physical and mental best. You, no doubt, have your own methods of getting into an exam-taking mood and keeping "in shape." The next section lists some ideas on this subject.

IV. KINDS OF QUESTIONS

Only rarely is the "essay" question, which you answer in narrative form, used in civil service tests. Civil service tests are usually of the short-answer type. Full instructions for answering these questions will be given to you at the examination. But in case this is your first experience with short-answer questions and separate answer sheets, here is what you need to know:

1) Multiple-choice Questions

Most popular of the short-answer questions is the "multiple choice" or "best answer" question. It can be used, for example, to test for factual knowledge, ability to solve problems or judgment in meeting situations found at work.

A multiple-choice question is normally one of three types—
- It can begin with an incomplete statement followed by several possible endings. You are to find the one ending which *best* completes the statement, although some of the others may not be entirely wrong.
- It can also be a complete statement in the form of a question which is answered by choosing one of the statements listed.

- It can be in the form of a problem – again you select the best answer.

Here is an example of a multiple-choice question with a discussion which should give you some clues as to the method for choosing the right answer:

When an employee has a complaint about his assignment, the action which will *best* help him overcome his difficulty is to
- A. discuss his difficulty with his coworkers
- B. take the problem to the head of the organization
- C. take the problem to the person who gave him the assignment
- D. say nothing to anyone about his complaint

In answering this question, you should study each of the choices to find which is best. Consider choice "A" – Certainly an employee may discuss his complaint with fellow employees, but no change or improvement can result, and the complaint remains unresolved. Choice "B" is a poor choice since the head of the organization probably does not know what assignment you have been given, and taking your problem to him is known as "going over the head" of the supervisor. The supervisor, or person who made the assignment, is the person who can clarify it or correct any injustice. Choice "C" is, therefore, correct. To say nothing, as in choice "D," is unwise. Supervisors have and interest in knowing the problems employees are facing, and the employee is seeking a solution to his problem.

2) True/False Questions

The "true/false" or "right/wrong" form of question is sometimes used. Here a complete statement is given. Your job is to decide whether the statement is right or wrong.

SAMPLE: A roaming cell-phone call to a nearby city costs less than a non-roaming call to a distant city.

This statement is wrong, or false, since roaming calls are more expensive.

This is not a complete list of all possible question forms, although most of the others are variations of these common types. You will always get complete directions for answering questions. Be sure you understand *how* to mark your answers – ask questions until you do.

V. RECORDING YOUR ANSWERS

Computer terminals are used more and more today for many different kinds of exams.

For an examination with very few applicants, you may be told to record your answers in the test booklet itself. Separate answer sheets are much more common. If this separate answer sheet is to be scored by machine – and this is often the case – it is highly important that you mark your answers correctly in order to get credit.

An electronic scoring machine is often used in civil service offices because of the speed with which papers can be scored. Machine-scored answer sheets must be marked with a pencil, which will be given to you. This pencil has a high graphite content which responds to the electronic scoring machine. As a matter of fact, stray dots may register as answers, so do not let your pencil rest on the answer sheet while you are pondering the correct answer. Also, if your pencil lead breaks or is otherwise defective, ask for another.

Since the answer sheet will be dropped in a slot in the scoring machine, be careful not to bend the corners or get the paper crumpled.

The answer sheet normally has five vertical columns of numbers, with 30 numbers to a column. These numbers correspond to the question numbers in your test booklet. After each number, going across the page are four or five pairs of dotted lines. These short dotted lines have small letters or numbers above them. The first two pairs may also have a "T" or "F" above the letters. This indicates that the first two pairs only are to be used if the questions are of the true-false type. If the questions are multiple choice, disregard the "T" and "F" and pay attention only to the small letters or numbers.

Answer your questions in the manner of the sample that follows:

32. The largest city in the United States is
    A. Washington, D.C.
    B. New York City
    C. Chicago
    D. Detroit
    E. San Francisco

1) Choose the answer you think is best. (New York City is the largest, so "B" is correct.)
2) Find the row of dotted lines numbered the same as the question you are answering. (Find row number 32)
3) Find the pair of dotted lines corresponding to the answer. (Find the pair of lines under the mark "B.")
4) Make a solid black mark between the dotted lines.

VI. BEFORE THE TEST

Common sense will help you find procedures to follow to get ready for an examination. Too many of us, however, overlook these sensible measures. Indeed, nervousness and fatigue have been found to be the most serious reasons why applicants fail to do their best on civil service tests. Here is a list of reminders:

- Begin your preparation early – Don't wait until the last minute to go scurrying around for books and materials or to find out what the position is all about.
- Prepare continuously – An hour a night for a week is better than an all-night cram session. This has been definitely established. What is more, a night a week for a month will return better dividends than crowding your study into a shorter period of time.
- Locate the place of the exam – You have been sent a notice telling you when and where to report for the examination. If the location is in a different town or otherwise unfamiliar to you, it would be well to inquire the best route and learn something about the building.
- Relax the night before the test – Allow your mind to rest. Do not study at all that night. Plan some mild recreation or diversion; then go to bed early and get a good night's sleep.
- Get up early enough to make a leisurely trip to the place for the test – This way unforeseen events, traffic snarls, unfamiliar buildings, etc. will not upset you.
- Dress comfortably – A written test is not a fashion show. You will be known by number and not by name, so wear something comfortable.

- Leave excess paraphernalia at home – Shopping bags and odd bundles will get in your way. You need bring only the items mentioned in the official notice you received; usually everything you need is provided. Do not bring reference books to the exam. They will only confuse those last minutes and be taken away from you when in the test room.
- Arrive somewhat ahead of time – If because of transportation schedules you must get there very early, bring a newspaper or magazine to take your mind off yourself while waiting.
- Locate the examination room – When you have found the proper room, you will be directed to the seat or part of the room where you will sit. Sometimes you are given a sheet of instructions to read while you are waiting. Do not fill out any forms until you are told to do so; just read them and be prepared.
- Relax and prepare to listen to the instructions
- If you have any physical problem that may keep you from doing your best, be sure to tell the test administrator. If you are sick or in poor health, you really cannot do your best on the exam. You can come back and take the test some other time.

VII. AT THE TEST

The day of the test is here and you have the test booklet in your hand. The temptation to get going is very strong. Caution! There is more to success than knowing the right answers. You must know how to identify your papers and understand variations in the type of short-answer question used in this particular examination. Follow these suggestions for maximum results from your efforts:

1) Cooperate with the monitor

The test administrator has a duty to create a situation in which you can be as much at ease as possible. He will give instructions, tell you when to begin, check to see that you are marking your answer sheet correctly, and so on. He is not there to guard you, although he will see that your competitors do not take unfair advantage. He wants to help you do your best.

2) Listen to all instructions

Don't jump the gun! Wait until you understand all directions. In most civil service tests you get more time than you need to answer the questions. So don't be in a hurry. Read each word of instructions until you clearly understand the meaning. Study the examples, listen to all announcements and follow directions. Ask questions if you do not understand what to do.

3) Identify your papers

Civil service exams are usually identified by number only. You will be assigned a number; you must not put your name on your test papers. Be sure to copy your number correctly. Since more than one exam may be given, copy your exact examination title.

4) Plan your time

Unless you are told that a test is a "speed" or "rate of work" test, speed itself is usually not important. Time enough to answer all the questions will be provided, but this does not mean that you have all day. An overall time limit has been set. Divide the total time (in minutes) by the number of questions to determine the approximate time you have for each question.

5) Do not linger over difficult questions

If you come across a difficult question, mark it with a paper clip (useful to have along) and come back to it when you have been through the booklet. One caution if you do this – be sure to skip a number on your answer sheet as well. Check often to be sure that you have not lost your place and that you are marking in the row numbered the same as the question you are answering.

6) Read the questions

Be sure you know what the question asks! Many capable people are unsuccessful because they failed to *read* the questions correctly.

7) Answer all questions

Unless you have been instructed that a penalty will be deducted for incorrect answers, it is better to guess than to omit a question.

8) Speed tests

It is often better NOT to guess on speed tests. It has been found that on timed tests people are tempted to spend the last few seconds before time is called in marking answers at random – without even reading them – in the hope of picking up a few extra points. To discourage this practice, the instructions may warn you that your score will be "corrected" for guessing. That is, a penalty will be applied. The incorrect answers will be deducted from the correct ones, or some other penalty formula will be used.

9) Review your answers

If you finish before time is called, go back to the questions you guessed or omitted to give them further thought. Review other answers if you have time.

10) Return your test materials

If you are ready to leave before others have finished or time is called, take ALL your materials to the monitor and leave quietly. Never take any test material with you. The monitor can discover whose papers are not complete, and taking a test booklet may be grounds for disqualification.

VIII. EXAMINATION TECHNIQUES

1) Read the general instructions carefully. These are usually printed on the first page of the exam booklet. As a rule, these instructions refer to the timing of the examination; the fact that you should not start work until the signal and must stop work at a signal, etc. If there are any *special* instructions, such as a choice of questions to be answered, make sure that you note this instruction carefully.

2) When you are ready to start work on the examination, that is as soon as the signal has been given, read the instructions to each question booklet, underline any key words or phrases, such as *least, best, outline, describe* and the like. In this way you will tend to answer as requested rather than discover on reviewing your paper that you *listed without describing*, that you selected the *worst* choice rather than the *best* choice, etc.

3) If the examination is of the objective or multiple-choice type – that is, each question will also give a series of possible answers: A, B, C or D, and you are called upon to select the best answer and write the letter next to that answer on your answer paper – it is advisable to start answering each question in turn. There may be anywhere from 50 to 100 such questions in the three or four hours allotted and you can see how much time would be taken if you read through all the questions before beginning to answer any. Furthermore, if you come across a question or group of questions which you know would be difficult to answer, it would undoubtedly affect your handling of all the other questions.

4) If the examination is of the essay type and contains but a few questions, it is a moot point as to whether you should read all the questions before starting to answer any one. Of course, if you are given a choice – say five out of seven and the like – then it is essential to read all the questions so you can eliminate the two that are most difficult. If, however, you are asked to answer all the questions, there may be danger in trying to answer the easiest one first because you may find that you will spend too much time on it. The best technique is to answer the first question, then proceed to the second, etc.

5) Time your answers. Before the exam begins, write down the time it started, then add the time allowed for the examination and write down the time it must be completed, then divide the time available somewhat as follows:
   - If 3-1/2 hours are allowed, that would be 210 minutes. If you have 80 objective-type questions, that would be an average of 2-1/2 minutes per question. Allow yourself no more than 2 minutes per question, or a total of 160 minutes, which will permit about 50 minutes to review.
   - If for the time allotment of 210 minutes there are 7 essay questions to answer, that would average about 30 minutes a question. Give yourself only 25 minutes per question so that you have about 35 minutes to review.

6) The most important instruction is to *read each question* and make sure you know what is wanted. The second most important instruction is to *time yourself properly* so that you answer every question. The third most important instruction is to *answer every question*. Guess if you have to but include something for each question. Remember that you will receive no credit for a blank and will probably receive some credit if you write something in answer to an essay question. If you guess a letter – say "B" for a multiple-choice question – you may have guessed right. If you leave a blank as an answer to a multiple-choice question, the examiners may respect your feelings but it will not add a point to your score. Some exams may penalize you for wrong answers, so in such cases *only*, you may not want to guess unless you have some basis for your answer.

7) Suggestions
   a. Objective-type questions
      1. Examine the question booklet for proper sequence of pages and questions
      2. Read all instructions carefully
      3. Skip any question which seems too difficult; return to it after all other questions have been answered
      4. Apportion your time properly; do not spend too much time on any single question or group of questions

5. Note and underline key words – *all, most, fewest, least, best, worst, same, opposite*, etc.
6. Pay particular attention to negatives
7. Note unusual option, e.g., unduly long, short, complex, different or similar in content to the body of the question
8. Observe the use of "hedging" words – *probably, may, most likely,* etc.
9. Make sure that your answer is put next to the same number as the question
10. Do not second-guess unless you have good reason to believe the second answer is definitely more correct
11. Cross out original answer if you decide another answer is more accurate; do not erase until you are ready to hand your paper in
12. Answer all questions; guess unless instructed otherwise
13. Leave time for review

b. Essay questions
1. Read each question carefully
2. Determine exactly what is wanted. Underline key words or phrases.
3. Decide on outline or paragraph answer
4. Include many different points and elements unless asked to develop any one or two points or elements
5. Show impartiality by giving pros and cons unless directed to select one side only
6. Make and write down any assumptions you find necessary to answer the questions
7. Watch your English, grammar, punctuation and choice of words
8. Time your answers; don't crowd material

8) Answering the essay question

Most essay questions can be answered by framing the specific response around several key words or ideas. Here are a few such key words or ideas:

M's: manpower, materials, methods, money, management
P's: purpose, program, policy, plan, procedure, practice, problems, pitfalls, personnel, public relations

  a. Six basic steps in handling problems:
    1. Preliminary plan and background development
    2. Collect information, data and facts
    3. Analyze and interpret information, data and facts
    4. Analyze and develop solutions as well as make recommendations
    5. Prepare report and sell recommendations
    6. Install recommendations and follow up effectiveness

  b. Pitfalls to avoid
    1. *Taking things for granted* – A statement of the situation does not necessarily imply that each of the elements is necessarily true; for example, a complaint may be invalid and biased so that all that can be taken for granted is that a complaint has been registered

2. *Considering only one side of a situation* – Wherever possible, indicate several alternatives and then point out the reasons you selected the best one
3. *Failing to indicate follow up* – Whenever your answer indicates action on your part, make certain that you will take proper follow-up action to see how successful your recommendations, procedures or actions turn out to be
4. *Taking too long in answering any single question* – Remember to time your answers properly

IX. AFTER THE TEST

Scoring procedures differ in detail among civil service jurisdictions although the general principles are the same. Whether the papers are hand-scored or graded by machine we have described, they are nearly always graded by number. That is, the person who marks the paper knows only the number – never the name – of the applicant. Not until all the papers have been graded will they be matched with names. If other tests, such as training and experience or oral interview ratings have been given, scores will be combined. Different parts of the examination usually have different weights. For example, the written test might count 60 percent of the final grade, and a rating of training and experience 40 percent. In many jurisdictions, veterans will have a certain number of points added to their grades.

After the final grade has been determined, the names are placed in grade order and an eligible list is established. There are various methods for resolving ties between those who get the same final grade – probably the most common is to place first the name of the person whose application was received first. Job offers are made from the eligible list in the order the names appear on it. You will be notified of your grade and your rank as soon as all these computations have been made. This will be done as rapidly as possible.

People who are found to meet the requirements in the announcement are called "eligibles." Their names are put on a list of eligible candidates. An eligible's chances of getting a job depend on how high he stands on this list and how fast agencies are filling jobs from the list.

When a job is to be filled from a list of eligibles, the agency asks for the names of people on the list of eligibles for that job. When the civil service commission receives this request, it sends to the agency the names of the three people highest on this list. Or, if the job to be filled has specialized requirements, the office sends the agency the names of the top three persons who meet these requirements from the general list.

The appointing officer makes a choice from among the three people whose names were sent to him. If the selected person accepts the appointment, the names of the others are put back on the list to be considered for future openings.

That is the rule in hiring from all kinds of eligible lists, whether they are for typist, carpenter, chemist, or something else. For every vacancy, the appointing officer has his choice of any one of the top three eligibles on the list. This explains why the person whose name is on top of the list sometimes does not get an appointment when some of the persons lower on the list do. If the appointing officer chooses the second or third eligible, the No. 1 eligible does not get a job at once, but stays on the list until he is appointed or the list is terminated.

X. HOW TO PASS THE INTERVIEW TEST

The examination for which you applied requires an oral interview test. You have already taken the written test and you are now being called for the interview test – the final part of the formal examination.

You may think that it is not possible to prepare for an interview test and that there are no procedures to follow during an interview. Our purpose is to point out some things you can do in advance that will help you and some good rules to follow and pitfalls to avoid while you are being interviewed.

What is an interview supposed to test?

The written examination is designed to test the technical knowledge and competence of the candidate; the oral is designed to evaluate intangible qualities, not readily measured otherwise, and to establish a list showing the relative fitness of each candidate – as measured against his competitors – for the position sought. Scoring is not on the basis of "right" and "wrong," but on a sliding scale of values ranging from "not passable" to "outstanding." As a matter of fact, it is possible to achieve a relatively low score without a single "incorrect" answer because of evident weakness in the qualities being measured.

Occasionally, an examination may consist entirely of an oral test – either an individual or a group oral. In such cases, information is sought concerning the technical knowledges and abilities of the candidate, since there has been no written examination for this purpose. More commonly, however, an oral test is used to supplement a written examination.

Who conducts interviews?

The composition of oral boards varies among different jurisdictions. In nearly all, a representative of the personnel department serves as chairman. One of the members of the board may be a representative of the department in which the candidate would work. In some cases, "outside experts" are used, and, frequently, a businessman or some other representative of the general public is asked to serve. Labor and management or other special groups may be represented. The aim is to secure the services of experts in the appropriate field.

However the board is composed, it is a good idea (and not at all improper or unethical) to ascertain in advance of the interview who the members are and what groups they represent. When you are introduced to them, you will have some idea of their backgrounds and interests, and at least you will not stutter and stammer over their names.

What should be done before the interview?

While knowledge about the board members is useful and takes some of the surprise element out of the interview, there is other preparation which is more substantive. It *is* possible to prepare for an oral interview – in several ways:

1) Keep a copy of your application and review it carefully before the interview

This may be the only document before the oral board, and the starting point of the interview. Know what education and experience you have listed there, and the sequence and dates of all of it. Sometimes the board will ask you to review the highlights of your experience for them; you should not have to hem and haw doing it.

2) Study the class specification and the examination announcement

Usually, the oral board has one or both of these to guide them. The qualities, characteristics or knowledges required by the position sought are stated in these documents. They offer valuable clues as to the nature of the oral interview. For example, if the job involves supervisory responsibilities, the announcement will usually indicate that knowledge of modern supervisory methods and the qualifications of the candidate as a supervisor will be tested. If so, you can expect such questions, frequently in the form of a hypothetical situation which you are expected to solve. NEVER go into an oral without knowledge of the duties and responsibilities of the job you seek.

3) Think through each qualification required

Try to visualize the kind of questions you would ask if you were a board member. How well could you answer them? Try especially to appraise your own knowledge and background in each area, *measured against the job sought*, and identify any areas in which you are weak. Be critical and realistic – do not flatter yourself.

4) Do some general reading in areas in which you feel you may be weak

For example, if the job involves supervision and your past experience has NOT, some general reading in supervisory methods and practices, particularly in the field of human relations, might be useful. Do NOT study agency procedures or detailed manuals. The oral board will be testing your understanding and capacity, not your memory.

5) Get a good night's sleep and watch your general health and mental attitude

You will want a clear head at the interview. Take care of a cold or any other minor ailment, and of course, no hangovers.

What should be done on the day of the interview?

Now comes the day of the interview itself. Give yourself plenty of time to get there. Plan to arrive somewhat ahead of the scheduled time, particularly if your appointment is in the fore part of the day. If a previous candidate fails to appear, the board might be ready for you a bit early. By early afternoon an oral board is almost invariably behind schedule if there are many candidates, and you may have to wait. Take along a book or magazine to read, or your application to review, but leave any extraneous material in the waiting room when you go in for your interview. In any event, relax and compose yourself.

The matter of dress is important. The board is forming impressions about you – from your experience, your manners, your attitude, and your appearance. Give your personal appearance careful attention. Dress your best, but not your flashiest. Choose conservative, appropriate clothing, and be sure it is immaculate. This is a business interview, and your appearance should indicate that you regard it as such. Besides, being well groomed and properly dressed will help boost your confidence.

Sooner or later, someone will call your name and escort you into the interview room. *This is it.* From here on you are on your own. It is too late for any more preparation. But remember, you asked for this opportunity to prove your fitness, and you are here because your request was granted.

What happens when you go in?

The usual sequence of events will be as follows: The clerk (who is often the board stenographer) will introduce you to the chairman of the oral board, who will introduce you to the other members of the board. Acknowledge the introductions before you sit down. Do not be surprised if you find a microphone facing you or a stenotypist sitting by. Oral interviews are usually recorded in the event of an appeal or other review.

Usually the chairman of the board will open the interview by reviewing the highlights of your education and work experience from your application – primarily for the benefit of the other members of the board, as well as to get the material into the record. Do not interrupt or comment unless there is an error or significant misinterpretation; if that is the case, do not hesitate. But do not quibble about insignificant matters. Also, he will usually ask you some question about your education, experience or your present job – partly to get you to start talking and to establish the interviewing "rapport." He may start the actual questioning, or turn it over to one of the other members. Frequently, each member undertakes the questioning on a particular area, one in which he is perhaps most competent, so you can expect each member to participate in the examination. Because time is limited, you may also expect some rather abrupt switches in the direction the questioning takes, so do not be upset by it. Normally, a board member will not pursue a single line of questioning unless he discovers a particular strength or weakness.

After each member has participated, the chairman will usually ask whether any member has any further questions, then will ask you if you have anything you wish to add. Unless you are expecting this question, it may floor you. Worse, it may start you off on an extended, extemporaneous speech. The board is not usually seeking more information. The question is principally to offer you a last opportunity to present further qualifications or to indicate that you have nothing to add. So, if you feel that a significant qualification or characteristic has been overlooked, it is proper to point it out in a sentence or so. Do not compliment the board on the thoroughness of their examination – they have been sketchy, and you know it. If you wish, merely say, "No thank you, I have nothing further to add." This is a point where you can "talk yourself out" of a good impression or fail to present an important bit of information. Remember, *you close the interview yourself.*

The chairman will then say, "That is all, Mr. _____, thank you." Do not be startled; the interview is over, and quicker than you think. Thank him, gather your belongings and take your leave. Save your sigh of relief for the other side of the door.

How to put your best foot forward

Throughout this entire process, you may feel that the board individually and collectively is trying to pierce your defenses, seek out your hidden weaknesses and embarrass and confuse you. Actually, this is not true. They are obliged to make an appraisal of your qualifications for the job you are seeking, and they want to see you in your best light. Remember, they must interview all candidates and a non-cooperative candidate may become a failure in spite of their best efforts to bring out his qualifications. Here are 15 suggestions that will help you:

1) Be natural – Keep your attitude confident, not cocky

If you are not confident that you can do the job, do not expect the board to be. Do not apologize for your weaknesses, try to bring out your strong points. The board is interested in a positive, not negative, presentation. Cockiness will antagonize any board member and make him wonder if you are covering up a weakness by a false show of strength.

2) Get comfortable, but don't lounge or sprawl

Sit erectly but not stiffly. A careless posture may lead the board to conclude that you are careless in other things, or at least that you are not impressed by the importance of the occasion. Either conclusion is natural, even if incorrect. Do not fuss with your clothing, a pencil or an ashtray. Your hands may occasionally be useful to emphasize a point; do not let them become a point of distraction.

3) Do not wisecrack or make small talk

This is a serious situation, and your attitude should show that you consider it as such. Further, the time of the board is limited – they do not want to waste it, and neither should you.

4) Do not exaggerate your experience or abilities

In the first place, from information in the application or other interviews and sources, the board may know more about you than you think. Secondly, you probably will not get away with it. An experienced board is rather adept at spotting such a situation, so do not take the chance.

5) If you know a board member, do not make a point of it, yet do not hide it

Certainly you are not fooling him, and probably not the other members of the board. Do not try to take advantage of your acquaintanceship – it will probably do you little good.

6) Do not dominate the interview

Let the board do that. They will give you the clues – do not assume that you have to do all the talking. Realize that the board has a number of questions to ask you, and do not try to take up all the interview time by showing off your extensive knowledge of the answer to the first one.

7) Be attentive

You only have 20 minutes or so, and you should keep your attention at its sharpest throughout. When a member is addressing a problem or question to you, give him your undivided attention. Address your reply principally to him, but do not exclude the other board members.

8) Do not interrupt

A board member may be stating a problem for you to analyze. He will ask you a question when the time comes. Let him state the problem, and wait for the question.

9) Make sure you understand the question

Do not try to answer until you are sure what the question is. If it is not clear, restate it in your own words or ask the board member to clarify it for you. However, do not haggle about minor elements.

10) Reply promptly but not hastily

A common entry on oral board rating sheets is "candidate responded readily," or "candidate hesitated in replies." Respond as promptly and quickly as you can, but do not jump to a hasty, ill-considered answer.

11) Do not be peremptory in your answers

A brief answer is proper – but do not fire your answer back. That is a losing game from your point of view. The board member can probably ask questions much faster than you can answer them.

12) Do not try to create the answer you think the board member wants

He is interested in what kind of mind you have and how it works – not in playing games. Furthermore, he can usually spot this practice and will actually grade you down on it.

13) Do not switch sides in your reply merely to agree with a board member

Frequently, a member will take a contrary position merely to draw you out and to see if you are willing and able to defend your point of view. Do not start a debate, yet do not surrender a good position. If a position is worth taking, it is worth defending.

14) Do not be afraid to admit an error in judgment if you are shown to be wrong

The board knows that you are forced to reply without any opportunity for careful consideration. Your answer may be demonstrably wrong. If so, admit it and get on with the interview.

15) Do not dwell at length on your present job

The opening question may relate to your present assignment. Answer the question but do not go into an extended discussion. You are being examined for a *new* job, not your present one. As a matter of fact, try to phrase ALL your answers in terms of the job for which you are being examined.

Basis of Rating

Probably you will forget most of these "do's" and "don'ts" when you walk into the oral interview room. Even remembering them all will not ensure you a passing grade. Perhaps you did not have the qualifications in the first place. But remembering them will help you to put your best foot forward, without treading on the toes of the board members.

Rumor and popular opinion to the contrary notwithstanding, an oral board wants you to make the best appearance possible. They know you are under pressure – but they also want to see how you respond to it as a guide to what your reaction would be under the pressures of the job you seek. They will be influenced by the degree of poise you display, the personal traits you show and the manner in which you respond.

ABOUT THIS BOOK

This book contains tests divided into Examination Sections. Go through each test, answering every question in the margin. We have also attached a sample answer sheet at the back of the book that can be removed and used. At the end of each test look at the answer key and check your answers. On the ones you got wrong, look at the right answer choice and learn. Do not fill in the answers first. Do not memorize the questions and answers, but understand the answer and principles involved. On your test, the questions will likely be different from the samples. Questions are changed and new ones added. If you understand these past questions you should have success with any changes that arise. Tests may consist of several types of questions. We have additional books on each subject should more study be advisable or necessary for you. Finally, the more you study, the better prepared you will be. This book is intended to be the last thing you study before you walk into the examination room. Prior study of relevant texts is also recommended. NLC publishes some of these in our Fundamental Series. Knowledge and good sense are important factors in passing your exam. Good luck also helps. So now study this Passbook, absorb the material contained within and take that knowledge into the examination. Then do your best to pass that exam.

EXAMINATION SECTION

EXAMINATION SECTION

TEST 1

DIRECTIONS: Each question or incomplete statement is followed by several suggested answers or completions. Select the one that BEST answers the question or completes the statement. *PRINT THE LETTER OF THE CORRECT ANSWER IN THE SPACE AT THE RIGHT.*

1. If a Private Patrol Operator wishes to work armed, how much insurance coverage is he/she required to carry?
   A. $250,000 B. $500,000 C. $1,000,000 D. $2,000,000

   1._____

2. If the vehicle of a Private Patrol Operator is equipped with an amber lightbar, how much must this vehicle be marked?
   A. Company name on doors and rear
   B. Company name on side doors, security on the rear
   C. Company logo on sides, PPO license number on rear
   D. Private Security or Security Patrol on both sides and on rear

   2._____

3. How many hours of training must a Private Patrol Operator undergo if he/she wants to carry tear gas or other chemical spray?
   A. 2 B. 4 C. 6 D. 8

   3._____

4. A Private Patrol Operator is required to keep the I-9 form of an ex-employee for what period of time?
   A. One year after the end of employment
   B. Three years after the end of employment
   C. Whichever is longer: three years from hire date or year from exit date
   D. Whichever is longer: five years from hire date or three years from exit date

   4._____

5. If a Private Patrol Operator changes residence address or business address, they must notify the Bureau of Security and Investigative Services within a time period of _____ days.
   A. 10 B. 30 C. 60 D. 90

   5._____

6. A firearms qualification card expires at a time period of _____ year(s) from the date of issuance if not renewed.
   A. 1 B. 2 C. 3 D. 5

   6._____

7. The fine for a misdemeanor violation of offering Private Patrol Operator services without a Private Patrol Operator license is what dollar amount?
   A. $1,000 B. $5,000 C. $10,000 D. $20,000

   7._____

8. Carrying a gun concealed under a shirt is usually what type of crime?
   A. Felony B. Misdemeanor
   C. Summary offense D. Inchoate crime

   8._____

9. Carrying a set of "brass knuckles" in your pocket is usually what type of crime?
   A. Felony
   B. Misdemeanor
   C. Summary offense
   D. Inchoate crime

10. If a person is convicted of providing Private Patrol Operator services without a license, he/she cannot be issued a Private Patrol Operator license for what time period following a conviction?
    A. 90 days
    B. 120 days
    C. 6 months
    D. 12 months

11. If a person is convicted a second time for providing Private Patrol Operator services without a license, he/she cannot be issued a PPO license for what period of time following the second conviction?
    A. 3 years
    B. 5 years
    C. 10 years
    D. 15 years

12. What is the fine if a Private Patrol Operator license is not properly posted?
    A. $250
    B. $500
    C. $1,000
    D. $2,500

13. The shoulder patch required to be on a Private Patrol Operator's security uniform must bear what two pieces of information?
    A. The words "Private Security" and the guard's name
    B. The guard's name and identification number
    C. The words "Private Security" and the guard's identification number
    D. The words "Private Security" and the name of the private patrol company the guard represents

14. In order to become a Private Patrol Operator, applicants should meet what minimum experience requirement?
    _____ of experience as a patrol person, guard, or watchman
    A. 6 months
    B. 1 year
    C. 2 years
    D. 3 years

15. If a Private Patrol Operator or an employee of a Private Patrol Operator discharges a firearm with the scope and course of his/her duty, a report of the incident must be provided to the Director of BSIS within what time frame?
    A. 24 hours
    B. 3 days
    C. 5 days
    D. 7 days

16. A Private Patrol Operator's application for a Private Patrol Operator license is considered to be "abandoned" if not completed within what time period of it being initially filed?
    A. 30 days
    B. 6 days
    C. 90 days
    D. 1 year

17. What is the MINIMUM number of hours of instruction required for a baton class?
    A. 4
    B. 6
    C. 8
    D. 12

18. If a guard quits working for a Private Patrol Operator without giving notice, when must the guard be given his/her final pay?
    A. Immediately
    B. Within 72 hours
    C. Within 7 days
    D. On the next scheduled payday

19. If a guard working for a Private Patrol Operator is fired by the Private Patrol Operator, when must the guard be given his/her final pay?
    A. Immediately
    B. Within 72 hours
    C. Within 7 days
    D. On the next scheduled payday

    19.____

20. Private Patrol Operator vehicles bearing amber colored lights must have markings in a size in which they are legible from a distance of _____ feet.
    A. 10
    B. 25
    C. 50
    D. 100

    20.____

21. What is the MAXIMUM time frame in which a Private Patrol Operator license can be expired and still be eligible for renewal?
    A. 30 days
    B. 1 year
    C. 2 years
    D. 3 years

    21.____

22. How many employees (or more) must a Private Patrol Operator company have in order for supervisors to be required by law to attend sexual harassment training?
    A. 5
    B. 10
    C. 25
    D. 50

    22.____

23. How often and for what time period is sexual harassment training required for supervisors who are required to attend?
    A. 2 hours every year
    B. 2 hours every 2 years
    C. 4 hours every 2 years
    D. 8 hours every 2 years

    23.____

24. Which of the following roles is required when advertising for another location, or conducting business from, other than the Private Patrol Operator's primary business location?
    A. Branch officer
    B. Exclusive officer
    C. Proprietary officer
    D. Managing officer

    24.____

25. How many employees can a Private Patrol Operator employ before being required to have a workers' compensation insurance policy?
    A. 0
    B. 5
    C. 10
    D. 50

    25.____

KEY (CORRECT ANSWERS)

1.	C	11.	B
2.	D	12.	A
3.	A	13.	D
4.	C	14.	B
5.	B	15.	D
6.	B	16.	D
7.	C	17.	C
8.	B	18.	B
9.	A	19.	A
10.	D	20.	C

21. D
22. D
23. B
24. A
25. A

TEST 2

DIRECTIONS: Each question or incomplete statement is followed by several suggested answers or completions. Select the one that BEST answers the question or completes the statement. *PRINT THE LETTER OF THE CORRECT ANSWER IN THE SPACE AT THE RIGHT.*

1. If a Private Patrol Operator dies, for what time period may the Private Patrol Operator's immediate family operate the business of the deceased Private Patrol Operator? 1.____
   A. 7 days B. 30 days C. 90 days D. 120 days

2. What is the proper name for an arrest made by a guard? 2.____
   A. Citizen's arrest B. Certified arrest
   C. Personal arrest D. Private person arrest

3. What IRS form would you use to report payments made to a regular employee? 3.____
   A. I-9 B. W-2 C. W-4 D. W-9

4. What type of form would be used by the employer to verify an employee's identity and to establish that the worker is eligible to accept employment in the United States? 4.____
   A. I-9 B. W-2 C. W-4 D. W-9

5. If a guard discharges his/her firearm while on duty, within what time period must the guard report this to his/her employer? 5.____
   A. 24 hours B. 3 days C. 5 days D. 7 days

6. During the initial 40 hours of training for a new guard, _____ hours should be devoted to terrorism awareness and weapons of mass destruction. 6.____
   A. 2 B. 4 C. 6 D. 8

7. A Type _____ extinguisher would be used on an electrical fire. 7.____
   A. A B. B C. C D. D

8. What self-defense weapon can a guard carry with no permit required? 8.____
   A. Tear gas B. Baton
   C. Electrical stun gun D. Unconcealed pistol

9. What penalty may a Private Patrol Operator incur if he/she has been found to have committed "dishonesty" or "fraud"? 9.____
   A. $250 fine
   B. Up to a year of incarceration
   C. More than a year of incarceration
   D. Suspension or revocation of the PPO license

10. If a person is hyperventilating, is unresponsive to touch, has cold skin, and is extremely talkative, what medical condition is this person likely experiencing?
    A. Shock
    B. Cardiac arrest
    C. Asthma attack
    D. Hypoglycemia

11. What IRS form is used by many Private Patrol Operators in a fraudulent attempt to get around laws involving payroll taxes and workers compensation insurance?
    A. I-9
    B. W-4
    C. W-9
    D. 1099

12. If a representative of a Private Patrol Operator company is involved in any way in the unlawful listening or recording of telephone calls, which of the following has he/she violated?
    A. Personal privacy
    B. PPO Code of Ethics
    C. Law enforcement regulations
    D. State and federal laws

13. What two cards must a security officer have in his/her possession while carrying a firearm on duty?
    A. Driver's license and guard card
    B. Driver's license and FQ card
    C. Guard card and FQ card
    D. Guard card and Social Security card

14. What equipment is NOT permitted to be a part of a security company's vehicles?
    A. Cellular phones
    B. Distinctive markings
    C. Amber lights
    D. Sirens

15. What are the counter-terrorism techniques known as "The 4 D's" that can be performed by a security guard?
    Deter,
    A. delay, deny, and detect
    B. distinguish, detract, and delay
    C. distinguish, deny, and delay
    D. detract, defense, and deny

16. Companies with how many employees are permitted to have oral and not written emergency action plans?
    A. 0-10
    B. 10-25
    C. 26-50
    D. 51 or more

17. Why is it required to report new employees or re-hired employees to the State?
    A. So employee time counts toward Social Security benefits
    B. So employee can be required to pay taxes
    C. So the employee can no longer be counted in unemployment statistics
    D. So the employee can be made responsible for unpaid child support

18. If a Private Patrol Operator or a security officer wants to obtain an exposed-weapon FQ firearms-carry card, how many hours of training are required?
    A. 8
    B. 14
    C. 20
    D. 40

19. What are the three main parts of basic protective measures?
    A. Rescue, alarm, and contain
    B. Promote, prevent, protect
    C. Time, distance, and shielding
    D. Knowledge, planning, execution

20. What is the first line of defense for all emergency situations?
    A. Reaction   B. Preparation   C. Evacuation   D. Leadership

21. All of the following items of information are included on a Firearm Carry card issued from the Bureau of Security and Investigative Services EXCEPT
    A. applicant's name
    B. Caliber of weapon
    C. Expiration date
    D. Applicant's Social Security number

22. What government agency has the ability to fine a Private Patrol Operator for I-0 non-compliance?
    A. Department of Labor
    B. Department of Homeland Security
    C. Occupational Safety and Health Administration
    D. Environmental Protection Agency

23. A security officer has all of the following in his/her possession in order to be hired on the spot by a Private Patrol Operator EXCEPT
    A. current identification
    B. current guard card
    C. current driver's license
    D. legal lability to work in the United States

24. What is the name of the legal document a Private Patrol Operator should obtain from a client and give photocopies of it to on-site guards, that allows towing companies to tow away illegally parked vehicles on the client's private property?
    A. Advance directive
    B. Power of attorney
    C. Right to privacy
    D. Proof of ownership

25. A law enforcement agent inducing a person to commit an offense that the person would otherwise have been unlikely to commit may be found guilty of which of the following?
    A. Coercion
    B. Entrapment
    C. Collusion
    D. Insubordination

KEY (CORRECT ANSWERS)

1.	D	11.	D
2.	D	12.	D
3.	B	13.	C
4.	A	14.	D
5.	A	15.	A
6.	B	16.	A
7.	C	17.	D
8.	C	18.	B
9.	D	19.	C
10.	A	20.	B

21. D
22. B
23. C
24. B
25. B

———

TEST 3

DIRECTIONS: Each question or incomplete statement is followed by several suggested answers or completions. Select the one that BEST answers the question or completes the statement. *PRINT THE LETTER OF THE CORRECT ANSWER IN THE SPACE AT THE RIGHT.*

1. The application and examination fee for an original Private Patrol Operator license may NOT exceed what dollar amount? 1.____
   A. $100   B. $250   C. $500   D. $1,000

2. A registration fee for a guard may NOT exceed what dollar amount? 2.____
   A. $10   B. $25   C. $50   D. $100

3. Who has the ultimate authority over what badge a Private Patrol Operator and his/her guards use when working? 3.____
   A. Local law enforcement
   B. Department of Homeland Security
   C. Occupational Safety and Health Administration
   D. Bureau of Security and Investigative Services

4. What agency regulates guard choices such as uniform color, badge types, and shoulder patches? 4.____
   A. Department of Labor
   B. Department of Homeland Security
   C. Occupational Safety and Health Administration
   D. Bureau of Security and Investigative Services

5. What state agency regulates employee-pay issues? 5.____
   A. Department of Labor
   B. Department of Industrial Relations
   C. Occupational Safety and Health Administration
   D. Bureau of Security and Investigative Services

6. Type _____ is a type of fire extinguisher used on a paper or wood fire. 6.____
   A. A   B. B   C. C   D. D

7. How many hours of CPR/first aid training does BSIS advise for a security officer? 7.____
   A. 2   B. 4   C. 6   D. 8

8. Type _____ is a type of fire extinguisher used on a liquid fire. 8.____
   A. A   B. B   C. C   D. D

9. Which of the following is permitted to carry a baton without a BSIS permit? 9.____
   A. Branch officer   B. Qualified manager
   C. Proprietary officer   D. Peace officer

10. A _____ arrest refers to a person being held in custody without probable cause or without an order issued by a court of competent jurisdiction.
    A. citizen's   B. certified   C. false   D. private person

11. If a firearm connected to a Private Patrol Operator or any of his/her staff becomes missing, or stolen while on duty, within what time frame must this be reported to local law enforcement?
    A. 24 hours   B. 3 days   C. 5 days   D. 7 days

12. What does the term "brandishing a weapon" mean?
    A. Carrying a concealed weapon
    B. Carrying an unconcealed weapon
    C. Carrying an unregistered weapon
    D. Drawing a weapon in a threatening manner

13. If a security officer is assigned to work a private party and someone uninvited attends and refuses to leave, what can the security officer do in this situation?
    A. Physically remove the person
    B. Arrest for trespass
    C. Arrest for disturbing the peace
    D. Hold the person at gunpoint until the peace officers arrive

14. All of the following should be included on a written report EXCEPT
    A. why it occurred
    B. where it occurred
    C. when it occurred
    D. witnesses to the occurrence

15. What agency requires companies such as construction sites, chemical companies, and refineries to have emergency action plans?
    A. Department of Labor
    B. Department of Industrial Relations
    C. Occupational Safety and Health Administration
    D. Bureau of Security and Investigative Services

16. When writing a proposal to a potential client, what is the MAIN item a Private Patrol Operator should be considering?
    A. Profit margin
    B. Needs of the client
    C. Fatigue of the protecting officers
    D. Environment needing to be protected

17. If a Private Patrol Operator allows one of his/her security officers to carry a baton without a permit, what fine should the PPO expect from BSIS?
    A. $1,000   B. $2,500   C. $5,000   D. $10,000

18. Penal Code _____ is a rule or law that allows a security officer to make an arrest.
    A. 187   B. 242   C. 459   D. 837

19. What IRS payroll form does an employee complete that tells how many exemptions that employee claims to have?
    A. I-9   B. W-4   C. W-9   D. 1099

20. If a Private Patrol Operator's Quality Manager resigns from the company, the non-QM PPO company owner must notify BSIS within _____ days.
    A. 7   B. 30   C. 60   D. 90

21. A guard should renew his/her guard card _____ days prior to the expiration date.
    A. 10-20   B. 30-45   C. 45-60   D. 60-90

22. A security officer can only frisk a person for being in possession of which of the following?
    A. Drugs   B. Money   C. Weapons   D. Stolen items

23. What is the rule on bullet capacity for semi-automatic pistols carried by guards and Private Patrol Operators?
    No more than _____ bullets.
    A. 6   B. 8   C. 10   D. 12

24. If a business wants to employ their own security officer instead of hiring a Private Patrol Operator to supply a guard, that business must register as a Proprietary Private Security Employer. What is the cost of this registration?
    A. $50   B. $75   C. $100   D. $250

25. Which of the following should never be kept in an employee's personnel file?
    A. W-4 form   B. I-9 form
    C. Employee resume   D. Performance evaluations

KEY (CORRECT ANSWERS)

1.	C	11.	D
2.	C	12.	D
3.	A	13.	B
4.	D	14.	A
5.	B	15.	C
6.	A	16.	A
7.	A	17.	B
8.	B	18.	D
9.	D	19.	B
10.	C	20.	B

21. D
22. C
23. C
24. B
25. B

TEST 4

DIRECTIONS: Each question or incomplete statement is followed by several suggested answers or completions. Select the one that BEST answers the question or completes the statement. *PRINT THE LETTER OF THE CORRECT ANSWER IN THE SPACE AT THE RIGHT.*

1. What document will a bank require you to present if you want a checking account in the name of your Private Patrol Operator company? 1._____
   A. Guard card
   B. I-9 form
   C. Company tax ID number
   D. Fictitious business name filing

2. If a Private Patrol Operator contracts with a K-12 school district, the guard has special training requirements if they are on the school campus more than how many hours per week? 2._____
   A. 10
   B. 20
   C. 30
   D. 40

3. What type of weapons of mass destruction is known to have trigger methods that can be chemical, electronic, or mechanical? 3._____
   A. Nuclear
   B. Chemical
   C. Biological
   D. Incendiary

4. What two conditions must be present before a suspect can be arrested for a felony? 4._____
   The felony must have been
   A. attempted and it must have been witnessed by another individual
   B. witnessed by the individual making the arrest and there must be evidence to support the arrest
   C. committed and there must be reasonable cause that the suspect actually committed the crime
   D. committed or attempted and there must be reasonable cause that the suspect actually committed the crime

5. Which of the following BEST describes the authority of a security guard to question an individual on his/her employer's private property? 5._____
   The security
   A. guard has the same rights as a private citizen when it comes to questioning others
   B. guard's right to question an individual is equivalent to the rights of a peace officer
   C. guard is not authorized to question an individual on his/her employer's property
   D. guard has the same right as his or her employer and more rights than that of a private citizen

6. Which of the following statements are TRUE regarding searching a suspect? 6._____
   A. Searching a suspect should be avoided
   B. Searches are performed to find evidence
   C. Suspects do not have rights in regards to being searched
   D. A search should be conducted before the suspect is placed under arrest

7. When is a security guard required to make an arrest?
   A. Anytime he/she witnesses a violation occurring
   B. When he/she witnesses an individual stealing merchandise
   C. When he/she witnesses a felony occur
   D. A security guard is never required to make an arrest

8. In order for a security guard to prevent offenses from occurring, he/she should be
   A. undercover
   B. highly visible
   C. creating diversions
   D. watching surveillance monitors

9. If you are the only security guard on duty and your assignment is to patrol a warehouse every night, you witness three men coming into the back of the warehouse with firearms.
   What should you do in this situation?
   A. Apprehend the three men and call the police
   B. Call the police but continue observing the men
   C. Go out the front door to save yourself from being seen
   D. Question the men and ask why they are entering the building

10. Smoking on public transportation and speeding are examples of which type of arrestable offense?
    A. Felony
    B. Infraction
    C. Malfeasance
    D. Misdemeanor

11. A registered employee, a Private Patrol Operator, or an alarm company may carry all of the following EXCEPT
    A. baton
    B. knife
    C. firearm
    D. simulated firearm

12. Mustard, cyanide, and chlorine are examples of what type of weapon of mass destruction?
    A. Nuclear
    B. Explosive
    C. Chemical
    D. Incendiary

13. What type of weapon of mass destruction creates fire and is easily made from home-made materials?
    A. Nuclear
    B. Explosive
    C. Chemical
    D. Incendiary

14. The reactionary distance that a security guard should keep between his/her adversary is _____ feet.
    A. 2-4
    B. 4-6
    C. 6-8
    D. 8-10

15. Which of the following offenses is punishable by a modest monetary fine?
    A. Felony
    B. Assault
    C. Infraction
    D. Misdemeanor

16. Which of the following statements are TRUE regarding the offense of trespass?
    A. It is a contract law offense and is always prosecuted.
    B. It is a civil offense and security officers cannot make an arrest.
    C. It is a criminal offense and only police officers can make an arrest.
    D. Security officers should immediately arrest trespassers and then hand them over to the police.

17. What should a security guard do if a site visitor refuses to be searched?
    A. Make an arrest and call the police
    B. Let them go but refuse admittance to the property
    C. Note the person's refusal but allow them onto the property
    D. Hold the person's property and call a manager for assistance

18. Assault is considered to be an offense of _____ law.
    A. tort   B. civil   C. contract   D. criminal

19. Which of the following must a security officer have in his/her possession at all times while on patrol?
    A. Site map
    B. Notebook
    C. Handcuffs
    D. Incident record book

20. In what circumstance might the use of force be deemed unreasonable? When it is used to
    A. make an arrest
    B. carry out a search
    C. prevent or stop a crime
    D. protect yourself or another individual

21. What is the FIRST thing an officer should do if unauthorized property is discovered during a search?
    A. Deny site access and hold on to the property in question
    B. File a police report but allow the person to retain the property
    C. Give the unauthorized property back but request off-site disposal
    D. Request to know why the person is in possession of the property

22. What is the security officer's FIRST priority when on patrol?
    A. Preserving site integrity
    B. Ensuring their own safety
    C. Ensuring the health and safety of others
    D. Preventing property loss and damage

23. Which of the following statements is TRUE regarding confidential information?
    A. It can be discussed with trusted friends, family, and co-workers.
    B. The consequences of disclosing such information can be serious.
    C. Disclosing such information to unauthorized persons is acceptable.
    D. Holding confidential information is unnecessary for a security officer.

24. Which of the following statements is TRUE regarding incident reports? 24.____
    A. The report must contain the home addresses of all parties involved.
    B. Signing and dating is the responsibility of the officer completing the report.
    C. At least one other security officer must witness incident report completion.
    D. It is acceptable for an officer not involved in the incident to complete the report.

25. When an arrest is required, which of the following must be provided to the individual under arrest? 25.____
    A. The location of their detainment
    B. Details regarding their statutory rights
    C. The reason for which they are being arrested
    D. Telephone access for calling legal representation

KEY (CORRECT ANSWERS)

1.	D	11.	D
2.	B	12.	C
3.	D	13.	D
4.	C	14.	C
5.	D	15.	C
6.	A	16.	C
7.	D	17.	B
8.	B	18.	D
9.	B	19.	B
10.	B	20.	B

21. D
22. B
23. B
24. B
25. B

EXAMINATION SECTION
TEST 1

DIRECTIONS: Each question or incomplete statement is followed by several suggested answers or completions. Select the one that BEST answers the question or completes the statement. *PRINT THE LETTER OF THE CORRECT ANSWER IN THE SPACE AT THE RIGHT.*

1. The officer who investigates accidents is always required to make a complete and accurate report.
   Of the following, the BEST reason for this procedure is to

   A. protect the operating agency against possible false claims
   B. provide a file of incidents which can be used as basic material for an accident prevention campaign
   C. provide the management with concrete evidence of violations of the rules by employees
   D. indicate what repairs need to be made

2. It is suggested that an officer keep all persons away from the area of an accident until an investigation has been completed.
   This suggested procedure is

   A. *good;* witnesses will be more likely to agree on a single story
   B. *bad;* such action blocks traffic flow and causes congestion
   C. *good;* objects of possible use as evidence will be protected from damage or loss
   D. *bad;* the flow of normal pedestrian traffic provides an opportunity for an investigator to determine the cause of the accident

3. A man having business with your agency is arguing with you and accuses you of being prejudiced against him. Although you explain to him that this is not so, he demands to see your supervisor.
   Of the following, the BEST course of action for you to take is to

   A. continue arguing with him until you have worn him out or convinced him
   B. take him to your supervisor
   C. ignore him and walk away from him to another part of the office
   D. escort him out of the office

4. An officer receives instructions from his supervisor which he does not fully understand.
   For the officer to ask for a further explanation would be

   A. *good;* chiefly because his supervisor will be impressed with his interest in his work
   B. *poor;* chiefly because the time of the supervisor will be needlessly wasted
   C. *good;* chiefly because proper performance depends on full understanding of the work to be done
   D. *poor;* chiefly because officers should be able to think for themselves

5. A person is making a complaint to an officer which seems unreasonable and of little importance.
   Of the following, the BEST action for the officer to take is to

A. criticize the person making the complaint for taking up his valuable time
B. laugh over the matter to show that the complaint is minor and silly
C. tell the person that anyone responsible for his grievance will be prosecuted
D. listen to the person making the complaint and tell him that the matter will be investigated

6. A member of the department shall not indulge in intoxicating liquor while in uniform. A member of the department is not required to wear a uniform, and a uniformed member while out of uniform shall not indulge in intoxicants to an extent unfitting him for duty.
Of the following, the MOST correct interpretation of this rule is that a

   A. member, off duty, not in uniform, may drink intoxicating liquor
   B. member, not on duty, but in uniform, may drink intoxicating liquor
   C. member, on duty, in uniform, may drink intoxicants
   D. uniformed member, in civilian clothes, may not drink intoxicants

7. You have a suggestion for an important change which you believe will improve a certain procedure in your agency. Of the following, the next course of action for you to take is to

   A. try it out yourself
   B. submit the suggestion to your immediate supervisor
   C. write a letter to the head of your agency asking for his approval
   D. wait until you are asked for suggestions before submitting this one

8. An officer shall study maps and literature concerning his assigned area and the streets and points of interest nearby.
Of the following, the BEST reason for this rule is that

   A. the officer will be better able to give correct information to persons desiring it
   B. the officer will be better able to drive a vehicle in the area
   C. the officer will not lose interest in his work
   D. supervisors will not need to train the officers in this subject

9. In asking a witness to a crime to identify a suspect, it is a common practice to place the suspect with a group of persons and ask the witness to pick out the person in question.
Of the following, the BEST reason for this practice is that it will

   A. make the identification more reliable than if the witness were shown the suspect alone
   B. protect the witness against reprisals
   C. make sure that the witness is telling the truth
   D. help select other participants in the crime at the same time

10. It is most important for all officers to obey the "Rules and Regulations" of their agency.
Of the following, the BEST reason for this statement is that

    A. supervisors will not need to train their new officers
    B. officers will never have to use their own judgment
    C. uniform procedures will be followed
    D. officers will not need to ask their supervisors for assistance

Questions 11-13.

DIRECTIONS: Answer questions 11 to 13 SOLELY on the basis of the following paragraph.

All members of the police force must recognize that the people, through their representatives, hire and pay the police and that, as in any other employment, there must exist a proper employer-employee relationship. The police officer must understand that the essence of a correct police attitude is a willingness to serve, but at the same time, he should distinguish between service and servility, and between courtesy and softness. He must be firm but also courteous, avoiding even an appearance of rudeness. He should develop a position that is friendly and unbiased, pleasant and sympathetic, in his relations with the general public, but firm and impersonal on occasions calling for regulation and control. A police officer should understand that his primary purpose is to prevent violations, not to arrest people. He should recognize the line of demarcation between a police function and passing judgment which is a court function. On the other side, a public that cooperates with the police, that supports them in their efforts and that observes laws and regulations, may be said to have a desirable attitude.

11. In accordance with this paragraph, the PROPER attitude for a police officer to take is to   11.____

    A. be pleasant and sympathetic at all times
    B. be friendly, firm, and impartial
    C. be stern and severe in meting out justice to all
    D. avoid being rude, except in those cases where the public is uncooperative

12. Assume that an officer is assigned by his superior officer to a busy traffic intersection and   12.____
    is warned to be on the lookout for motorists who skip the light or who are speeding.
    According to this paragraph, it would be proper for the officer in this assignment to

    A. give a summons to every motorist whose ear was crossing when the light changed
    B. hide behind a truck and wait for drivers who violate traffic laws
    C. select at random motorists who seem to be impatient and lecture them sternly on traffic safety
    D. stand on post in order to deter violations and give offenders a summons or a warning as required

13. According to this paragraph, a police officer must realize that the primary purpose of   13.____
    police work is to

    A. provide proper police service in a courteous manner
    B. decide whether those who violate the law should be punished
    C. arrest those who violate laws
    D. establish a proper employer-employee relationship

Questions 14-15.

DIRECTIONS: Answer questions 14 and 15 SOLELY on the basis of the following paragraph.

If a motor vehicle fails to pass inspection, the owner will be given a rejection notice by the inspection station. Repairs must be made within ten days after this notice is issued. It is not necessary to have the required adjustment or repairs made at the station where the inspection occurred. The vehicle may be taken to any other garage. Re-inspection after repairs may be made at any official inspection station, not necessarily the same station which made the initial inspection. The registration of any motor vehicle for which an inspection sticker has not been obtained as required, or which is not repaired and inspected within ten days after inspection indicates defects, is subject to suspension. A vehicle cannot be used on public highways while its registration is under suspension.

14. According to the above paragraph, the owner of a car which does NOT pass inspection must

    A. have repairs made at the same station which rejected his car
    B. take the car to another station and have it re-inspected
    C. have repairs made anywhere and then have the car re-inspected
    D. not use the car on a public highway until the necessary repairs have been made

14.____

15. According to the above paragraph, the one of the following which may be cause for suspension of the registration of a vehicle is that

    A. an inspection sticker was issued before the rejection notice had been in force for ten days
    B. it was not re-inspected by the station that rejected it originally
    C. it was not re-inspected either by the station that rejected it originally or by the garage which made the repairs
    D. it has not had defective parts repaired within ten days after inspection

15.____

Questions 16-20.

DIRECTIONS: Answer questions 16 to 20 SOLELY on the basis of the following paragraph.

If we are to study crime in its widest social setting, we will find a variety of conduct which, although criminal in the legal sense, is not offensive to the moral conscience of a considerable number of persons. Traffic violations, for example, do not brand the offender as guilty of moral offense. In fact, the recipient of a traffic ticket is usually simply the subject of some good-natured joking by his friends. Although there may be indignation among certain groups of citizens against gambling and liquor law violations, these activities are often tolerated, if not openly supported, by the more numerous residents of the community. Indeed, certain social and service clubs regularly conduct gambling games and lotteries for the purpose of raising funds. Some communities regard violations involving the sale of liquor with little concern in order to profit from increased license fees and taxes paid by dealers. The thousand and one forms of political graft and corruption which infest our urban centers only occasionally arouse public condemnation and official action.

16. According to the paragraph, all types of illegal conduct are

    A. condemned by all elements of the community
    B. considered a moral offense, although some are tolerated by a few citizens
    C. violations of the law, but some are acceptable to certain elements of the community
    D. found in a social setting which is not punishable by law

16.____

17. According to the paragraph, traffic violations are generally considered by society as

    A. crimes requiring the maximum penalty set by the law
    B. more serious than violations of the liquor laws

17.____

C. offenses against the morals of the community
D. relatively minor offenses requiring minimum punishment

18. According to the paragraph, a lottery conducted for the purpose of raising funds for a church

    A. is considered a serious violation of law
    B. may be tolerated by a community which has laws against gambling
    C. may be conducted under special laws demanded by the more numerous residents of a community
    D. arouses indignation in most communities

19. On the basis of the paragraph, the MOST likely reaction in the community to a police raid on a gambling casino would be

    A. more an attitude of indifference than interest in the raid
    B. general approval of the raid
    C. condemnation of the raid by most people
    D. demand for further action since this raid is not sufficient to end gambling activities

20. The one of the following which BEST describes the central thought of this paragraph and would be MOST suitable as a title for it is

    A. CRIME AND THE POLICE
    B. PUBLIC CONDEMNATION OF GRAFT AND CORRUPTION
    C. GAMBLING IS NOT ALWAYS A VICIOUS BUSINESS
    D. PUBLIC ATTITUDE TOWARD LAW VIOLATIONS

Questions 21-23.

DIRECTIONS: Answer questions 21 to 23 SOLELY on the basis of the following paragraph.

The law enforcement agency is one of the most important agencies in the field of juvenile delinquency prevention. This is so not because of the social work connected with this problem, however, for this is not a police matter, but because the officers are usually the first to come in contact with the delinquent. The manner of arrest and detention makes a deep impression upon him and affects his life-long attitude toward society and the law. The juvenile court is perhaps the most important agency in this work. Contrary to the general opinion, however, it is not primarily concerned with putting children into correctional schools. The main purpose of the juvenile court is to save the child and to develop his emotional make-up in order that he can grow up to be a decent and well-balanced citizen. The system of probation is the means whereby the court seeks to accomplish these goals.

21. According to this paragraph, police work is an important part of a program to prevent juvenile delinquency because

    A. social work is no longer considered important in juvenile delinquency prevention
    B. police officers are the first to have contact with the delinquent
    C. police officers jail the offender in order to be able to change his attitude toward society and the law
    D. it is the first step in placing the delinquent in jail

22. According to this paragraph, the CHIEF purpose of the juvenile court is to   22.____

    A. punish the child for his offense
    B. select a suitable correctional school for the delinquent
    C. use available means to help the delinquent become a better person
    D. provide psychiatric care for the delinquent

23. According to this paragraph, the juvenile court directs the development of delinquents   23.____
    under its care CHIEFLY by

    A. placing the child under probation
    B. sending the child to a correctional school
    C. keeping the delinquent in prison
    D. returning the child to his home

Questions 24-27.

DIRECTIONS: Answer questions 24 to 27 SOLELY on the basis of the following paragraph.

When a vehicle has been disabled in the tunnel, the officer on patrol in this zone shall press the EMERGENCY TRUCK light button. In the fast lane, red lights will go on throughout the tunnel; in the slow lane, amber lights will go on throughout the tunnel. The yellow zone light will go on at each signal control station throughout the tunnel and will flash the number of the zone in which the stoppage has occurred. A red flashing pilot light will appear only at the signal control station at which the EMERGENCY TRUCK button was pressed. The emergency garage will receive an audible and visual signal indicating the signal control station at which the EMERGENCY TRUCK button was pressed. The garage officer shall acknowledge receipt of the signal by pressing the acknowledgment button. This will cause the pilot light at the operated signal control station in the tunnel to cease flashing and to remain steady. It is an answer to the officer at the operated signal control station that the emergency truck is responding to the call.

24. According to this paragraph, when the EMERGENCY TRUCK light button is pressed,   24.____

    A. amber lights will go on in every lane throughout the tunnel
    B. emergency signal lights will go on only in the lane in which the disabled vehicle happens to be
    C. red lights will go on in the fast lane throughout the tunnel
    D. pilot lights at all signal control stations will turn amber

25. According to this paragraph, the number of the zone in which the stoppage has occurred   25.____
    is flashed

    A. immediately after all the lights in the tunnel turn red
    B. by the yellow zone light at each signal control station
    C. by the emergency truck at the point of stoppage
    D. by the emergency garage

26. According to this paragraph, an officer near the disabled vehicle will know that the emer-   26.____
    gency tow truck is coming when

    A. the pilot light at the operated signal control station appears and flashes red
    B. an audible signal is heard in the tunnel

C. the zone light at the operated signal control station turns red
D. the pilot light at the operated signal control station becomes steady

27. Under the system described in the paragraph, it would be CORRECT to come to the conclusion that

    A. officers at all signal control stations are expected to acknowledge that they have received the stoppage signal
    B. officers at all signal control stations will know where the stoppage has occurred
    C. all traffic in both lanes of that side of the tunnel in which the stoppage has occurred must stop until the emergency truck has arrived
    D. there are two emergency garages, each able to respond to stoppages in traffic going in one particular direction

Questions 28-30.

DIRECTIONS: Answer questions 28 to 30 SOLELY on the basis of the following paragraphs.

In cases of accident, it is most important for an officer to obtain the name, age, residence, occupation, and a full description of the person injured, names and addresses of witnesses. He shall also obtain a statement of the attendant circumstances. He shall carefully note contributory conditions, if any, such as broken pavement, excavation, tights not burning, snow and ice on the roadway, etc. He shall enter all facts in his memorandum book and on Form 17 or Form 18 and promptly transmit the original of the form to his superior officer and the duplicate to headquarters.

An officer shall render reasonable assistance to sick or injured persons. If the circumstances appear to require the services of a physician, he shall summon a physician by telephoning the superior officer on duty and notifying him of the apparent nature of the illness or accident and the location where the physician will be required. He may summon other officers to assist if circumstances warrant.

In case of an accident or where a person is sick on city property, an officer shall obtain the information necessary to fill out card Form 18 and record this in his memorandum book and promptly telephone the facts to his superior officer. He shall deliver the original card at the expiration of his tour to his superior officer and transmit the duplicate to headquarters.

28. According to this quotation, the MOST important consideration in any report on a case of accident or injury is to

    A. obtain all the facts
    B. telephone his superior officer at once
    C. obtain a statement of the attendant circumstances
    D. determine ownership of the property on which the accident occurred

29. According to this quotation, in the case of an accident on city property, the officer should always

    A. summon a physician before filling out any forms or making any entries in his memorandum book
    B. give his superior officer on duty a prompt report by telephone

C. immediately bring the original of Form 18 to his superior officer on duty
D. call at least one other officer to the scene to witness conditions

30. If the procedures stated in this quotation were followed for all accidents in the city, an impartial survey of accidents occurring during any period of time in this city may be MOST easily made by

   A. asking a typical officer to show you his memorandum book
   B. having a superior officer investigate whether contributory conditions mentioned by witnesses actually exist
   C. checking all the records of all superior officers
   D. checking the duplicate card files at headquarters

Questions 31-55.

DIRECTIONS: In each of questions 31 to 55, select the lettered word or phrase which means MOST NEARLY the same as the first word in the row.

31. RENDEZVOUS

   A. parade   B. neighborhood
   C. meeting place   D. wander about

32. EMINENT

   A. noted   B. rich   C. rounded   D. nearby

33. CAUSTIC

   A. cheap   B. sweet   C. evil   D. sharp

34. BARTER

   A. annoy   B. trade   C. argue   D. cheat

35. APTITUDE

   A. friendliness   B. talent
   C. conceit   D. generosity

36. PROTRUDE

   A. project   B. defend   C. choke   D. boast

37. FORTITUDE

   A. disposition   B. restlessness
   C. courage   D. poverty

38. PRELUDE

   A. introduction   B. meaning
   C. prayer   D. secret

39. SECLUSION

   A. primitive   B. influence
   C. imagination   D. privacy

40. RECTIFY
    A. correct   B. construct   C. divide   D. scold

41. TRAVERSE
    A. rotate   B. compose   C. train   D. cross

42. ALLEGE
    A. raise   B. convict   C. declare   D. chase

43. MENIAL
    A. pleasant   B. unselfish
    C. humble   D. stupid

44. DEPLETE
    A. exhaust   B. gather   C. repay   D. close

45. ERADICATE
    A. construct   B. advise   C. destroy   D. exclaim

46. CAPITULATE
    A. cover   B. surrender   C. receive   D. execute

47. RESTRAIN
    A. restore   B. drive   C. review   D. limit

48. AMALGAMATE
    A. join   B. force   C. correct   D. clash

49. DEJECTED
    A. beaten   B. speechless
    C. weak   D. low-spirited

50. DETAIN
    A. hide   B. accuse   C. hold   D. mislead

KEY (CORRECT ANSWERS)

1. A	11. B	21. B	31. C	41. D
2. C	12. D	22. C	32. A	42. C
3. B	13. A	23. A	33. D	43. C
4. C	14. C	24. C	34. B	44. A
5. D	15. D	25. B	35. B	45. C
6. A	16. C	26. D	36. A	46. B
7. B	17. D	27. B	37. C	47. D
8. A	18. B	28. A	38. A	48. A
9. A	19. A	29. B	39. D	49. D
10. C	20. D	30. D	40. A	50. C

TEST 2

DIRECTIONS: Each question or incomplete statement is followed by several suggested answers or completions. Select the one that BEST answers the question or completes the statement. *PRINT THE LETTER OF THE CORRECT ANSWER IN THE SPACE AT THE RIGHT.*

1. AMPLE
   A. necessary   B. plentiful   C. protected   D. tasty

   1.____

2. EXPEDITE
   A. sue   B. omit   C. hasten   D. verify

   2.____

3. FRAGMENT
   A. simple tool   B. broken part
   C. basic outline   D. weakness

   3.____

4. ADVERSARY
   A. thief   B. partner   C. loser   D. foe

   4.____

5. ACHIEVE
   A. accomplish   B. begin   C. develop   D. urge

   5.____

Questions 6-10.

DIRECTIONS: Answer Questions 6 to 10 on the basis of the information given in the table on the following page. The numbers which have been omitted from the table can be calculated from the other numbers which are given.

NUMBER OF DWELLING UNITS CONSTRUCTED

Year	Private one-family houses	In private apt. houses	In public housing	Total dwelling units
1996	4,500	500	600	5,600
1997	9,200	5,300	2,800	17,300
1998	8,900	12,800	6,800	28,500
1999	12,100	15,500	7,100	34,700
2000	?	12,200	14,100	39,200
2001	10,200	26,000	8,600	44,800
2002	10,300	17,900	7,400	35,600
2003	11,800	18,900	7,700	38,400
2004	12,700	22,100	8,400	43,200
2005	13,300	24,300	8,100	45,700
TOTALS	105,900	?	?	?

6. According to this table, the average number of public housing units constructed yearly during the period 1996 through 2005 was

   A. 7,160   B. 6,180   C. 7,610   D. 6,810

   6.____

7. Of the following, the two years in which the number of private one-family homes constructed was GREATEST for the two years together is

   A. 1998 and 1999
   B. 1997 and 2003
   C. 1998 and 2004
   D. 2001 and 2002

8. For the entire period of 1996 through 2005, the total of all private one-family houses constructed exceeded the total of all public housing units constructed by

   A. 34,300
   B. 45,700
   C. 50,000
   D. 83,900

9. Of the total number of private apartment house dwelling units constructed in the ten years given in the table, the percentage which was constructed in 2002 was MOST NEARLY

   A. 5%
   B. 11%
   C. 16%
   D. 21%

10. Considering dwelling units of all types, the average number constructed annually in the period from 2001 through 2005 was GREATER than the average number constructed annually in the period from 1996 through 2000 by

    A. 16,480
    B. 33,320
    C. 79,300
    D. 82,400

11. A car speeds through the toll entrance of a 2 1/4 mile long bridge without paying the toll and reaches the other end of the bridge 1 minute and 30 seconds later. The car was traveling MOST NEARLY at a rate of _____ miles per hour.

    A. 60
    B. 70
    C. 80
    D. 90

12. During one week, 21,500 vehicles passed through the toll booths of a certain bridge. Of these, 550 were buses, 2,230 were trucks, and the rest were passenger cars. The toll charges were $3.50 for a passenger car, $7 for a truck and $14 for a bus. The total income for the week was

    A. $80,850
    B. $88,830
    C. $102,550
    D. $109,550

13. A bullet fired from a revolver travels 100 feet the first second, and each succeeding second it travels a distance 10% less than during the immediately preceding second. The number of feet the bullet will have traveled at the end of the fourth second is MOST NEARLY

    A. 272
    B. 320
    C. 344
    D. 360

14. An officer receives a uniform allowance of $500 a year in a lump sum. Of this amount, he spends $180 for a winter jacket and 40% of the remainder for two pairs of trousers. The officer now wishes to buy a winter overcoat which costs $240.
    The percentage of the purchase price of the overcoat by which he will be short is

    A. 20%
    B. 25%
    C. 48%
    D. 60%

15. It has been suggested that small light cars can be used for certain kinds of police work. These light vehicles can run 30 miles per gallon of gasoline as contrasted with standard cars which run only 15 miles per gallon. Assume gasoline costs the city $3.75 per gallon. During 9,000 miles of travel, use of the small light car in preference to the standard car would result in a saving in gasoline costs of MOST NEARLY

    A. $1,125
    B. $1,500
    C. $1,875
    D. $2,250

16. Out of a total of 34,750 felony complaints in 2006, 14,200 involved burglary. In 2005, there was a total of 32,300 felony complaints of which 12,800 were burglary.
Of the increase in felonies from 2005 to 2006, the increase in burglaries comprised APPROXIMATELY

    A. 27%   B. 37%   C. 47%   D. 57%

17. A certain city department has two offices which issue permits, one office handling twice as many applicants as the other. The smaller office grants permits to 40% of its applicants. The larger office handling twice as many applicants grants permits to 60% of its applicants.
If there were 900 applicants at both offices together on a given day, the total number of permits granted by both offices would be MOST NEARLY

    A. 420   B. 450   C. 480   D. 510

18. If a co-worker is not breathing after receiving an electric shock but is no longer in contact with the electricity, it is MOST important for you to

    A. avoid moving him
    B. wrap the victim in a blanket
    C. start artificial respiration promptly
    D. force him to take hot liquids

19. Employees using supplies from one of the first-aid kits available throughout the building are required to submit an immediate report of the occurrence.
Logical reasoning shows that the MOST important reason for this report is so that the

    A. supplies used will be sure to be replaced
    B. first-aid kit can be properly sealed again
    C. employee will be credited for his action
    D. record of first-aid supplies will be up-to-date

20. The BEST IMMEDIATE first-aid treatment for a scraped knee is to

    A. apply plain vaseline   B. wash it with soap and water
    C. apply heat   D. use a knee splint

21. Artificial respiration after a severe electrical shock is ALWAYS necessary when the shock results in

    A. unconsciousness   B. stoppage of breathing
    C. bleeding   D. a burn

22. The authority gives some of its maintenance employees instruction in first aid.
The MOST likely reason for doing this is to

    A. eliminate the need for calling a doctor in case of accident
    B. provide temporary emergency treatment in case of accident
    C. lower the cost of accidents to the authority
    D. reduce the number of accidents

23. The BEST IMMEDIATE first aid if a chemical solution splashes into the eyes is to

    A. protect the eyes from the light by bandaging
    B. rub the eyes dry with a towel

C. cause tears to flow by staring at a bright light
D. flush the eyes with large quantities of clean water

24. If you had to telephone for an ambulance because of an accident, the MOST important information for you to give the person who answered the telephone would be the

   A. exact time of the accident
   B. cause of the accident
   C. place where the ambulance is needed
   D. names and addresses of those injured

25. If a person has a deep puncture wound in his finger caused by a sharp nail, the BEST IMMEDIATE first aid procedure would be to

   A. encourage bleeding by exerting pressure around the injured area
   B. stop all bleeding
   C. prevent air from reaching the wound
   D. probe the wound for steel particles

26. In addition to cases of submersion, artificial respiration is a recommended first aid procedure for

   A. sunstroke   B. electrical shock   C. chemical poisoning   D. apoplexy

27. Assume that you are called on to render first aid to a man injured in an accident. You find he is bleeding profusely, is unconscious, and has a broken arm. There is a strong odor of alcohol about him.
The FIRST thing for which you should treat him is the

   A. bleeding   B. unconsciousness   C. broken arm   D. alcoholism

28. In applying first aid for removal of a foreign body in the eye, an important precaution to be observed is NOT to

   A. attempt to wash out the foreign body
   B. bring the upper eyelid down over the lower
   C. rub the eye
   D. touch or attempt to remove a speck on the lower lid

29. The one of the following symptoms which is LEAST likely to indicate that a person involved in an accident requires first aid for shock is that

   A. he has fainted twice
   B. his face is red and flushed
   C. his skin is wet with sweat
   D. his pulse is rapid

30. When giving first aid to a person suffering from shock as a result of an auto accident, it is MOST important to

   A. massage him in order to aid blood circulation
   B. have him sip whiskey
   C. prop him up in a sitting position
   D. cover the person and keep him warm

Questions 31-34.

DIRECTIONS: Answer questions 31 to 34 SOLELY on the basis of the following paragraph.

Assume that you are an officer assigned to one large office which issues and receives applications for various permits and licenses. The office consists of one section where the necessary forms are issued; another section where fees are paid to a cashier; and desks where applicants are interviewed and their forms reviewed and completed. There is also a section containing tables and chairs where persons may sit and fill out their applications before being interviewed or paying the fees. your duties consist of answering simple questions, directing the public to the correct section of the office, and maintaining order.

31. A man who speaks English poorly asks you for assistance in obtaining and filling out an application for a permit. You should

    A. send him to an interviewer who can assist him
    B. try to determine what permit he wants and fill out the form for him
    C. refer the man to the office supervisor
    D. ask another applicant to help this person

31.____

32. The office becomes noisy and crowded, with people milling around waiting for service at the various sections.
Of the following, the BEST action for you to take is to

    A. stand in a prominent place and in a loud voice request the people to be quiet
    B. direct all the people not being served to wait at the unoccupied tables until you call them
    C. line up the people in front of each section and keep the lines in good order
    D. tell the people to form a single line outside the office and let in a few at a time

32.____

33. A man who has just been denied a permit becomes angry and shouts that if he "knew the right people" he too could get a permit. His behavior is disturbing the office.
Of the following, the BEST action for you to take is to

    A. order the man to leave at once since his business is done
    B. tell the man to be quiet and file another application
    C. suggest to the supervisor that a pamphlet be prepared explaining the requirements for permits in simple language
    D. ask an interviewer to explain the requirements for his permit to the person and his right of appeal

33.____

34. Just before the close of business, a man rushes in and insists on being interviewed for a permit because his present one expires that night.
Of the following, the BEST action for you to take is to

    A. tell the man that the office is closed
    B. tell the man that there will be no penalty if he returns early the next morning
    C. inquire if an interviewer is still available to take care of him and send him to that desk
    D. tell the cashier to collect the fee and tell the man to return the next morning for an interview

34.____

35. Fingerprints are often taken of applicants for licenses. Of the following, the MOST valid reason for this procedure is that

    A. the license of someone who commits a crime can be more readily revoked
    B. applicants can be checked for possible criminal records
    C. it helps to make sure that the proper license fee is paid
    D. a complete employment record of the applicant is obtained

36. Assume that an officer is on patrol at 2 A.M. He notices that the night light inside one of the stores in a public building is out. The store is locked.
    Of the following, the FIRST action for him to take at this time is to

    A. continue on his patrol since the light probably burned out
    B. enter the store by any means possible so he can check it
    C. report the matter to his superior
    D. shine his flashlight through the window to look for anything unusual

37. In questioning a man suspected of having committed a theft, the BEST procedure for an officer to follow is to

    A. induce the man to express his feelings about the police, the courts, and his home environment
    B. threaten him with beatings when he refuses to answer your questions
    C. make any promises necessary to get him to confess
    D. remain calm and objective

38. As an officer, you are on duty in one of the offices of a large public building. A woman who has just finished her business with this office comes to you and reports that her son who was with her is missing.
    The one of the following which is the BEST action for you to take FIRST is to

    A. tell the mother that the child is probably all right and ask her to go to the local police station for help in finding the boy
    B. suggest that the mother wait in the office until the child turns up
    C. check nearby offices in an attempt to locate the child
    D. telephone the local police station and ask if any reports fitting the description of the child have been received

39. An officer assigned to patrol inside a public building at night has observed two men standing outside the doorway. Of the following, the MOST appropriate action for the officer to take FIRST is to

    A. approach the two men and ask them why they are standing there
    B. hide and wait for the two men to take some action
    C. phone the local police station and ask for help since these men may be planning criminal action
    D. check all the entrance doors of the building to make sure that they are locked

40. It is standard practice for special officers to inspect the restrooms in public buildings. This is done at regular intervals while on patrol.
    Of the following, the BEST reason for this practice is to

    A. inspect sanitary conditions
    B. discourage loiterers and potential criminals

C. check the ventilation
D. determine if all the equipment and plumbing is working properly

41. While on duty in the evening as an officer assigned to a public building, you receive a report that a card game is going on in one of the offices. Gambling is forbidden on government property.
Of the following, the BEST course of action for you to take is to

    A. go to the office and order the card players to leave
    B. ignore the complaint since this is probably just harmless social card playing
    C. report the matter to the building manager the next day
    D. go to the office and, if warranted, issue an appropriate warning

42. It has been suggested that special officers establish good working relationships with the local police officers of the police department on duty in the neighborhood.
Of the following, the MOST valid reason for this practice is that

    A. a spirit of good feeling and high morale will be created among members of the police department
    B. local police officers will probably cooperate more readily with the special officer
    C. local police officers can take over the building patrol duties of the special officer in case he is absent
    D. special officers have an even stronger obligation than ordinary citizens to cooperate with the police

43. It has been proposed that an officer assigned to a public building at night remain at one location in the building, instead of walking on patrol through the building.
This proposal is

    A. *bad;* chiefly because the officer would probably sit instead of stand at the proper location
    B. *good;* chiefly because the officer could do a better job of watching the entire building from one point
    C. *bad;* chiefly because anyone seeking to enter the building for illegal purposes might be able to do so at a point other than where the special officer is on duty
    D. *good;* chiefly because his supervisors would know exactly where to find him

44. In a busy office, an officer has been assigned the duty of making sure that the public is served in the order of their arrival at the office and that some employee is always taking care of a person desiring help.
Of the following, the BEST method for the officer to follow is to

    A. line up the persons in the waiting room
    B. give a numbered ticket to each person waiting and call out the numbers, in order, when an employee becomes available
    C. loudly announce "next" when an employee is available to serve someone
    D. seat one person next to each employee's desk and let the others wait for the first vacant seat

45. Two men have broken into and entered a building at night. The officer on duty at this building sees them, chases them out, and then observes them in the adjoining building. Of the following, the BEST course of action for the officer to take is to

    A. notify the local police station and be ready to aid the police
    B. enter the adjoining building to find the men
    C. notify the manager of his own building
    D. continue on duty since these men have left the building for which he is responsible

46. While an officer is on duty in a crowded waiting room, he finds a woman's purse on the floor.
    Of the following, the FIRST course of action for him to take is to

    A. hold it up in the air, ask who owns it, and give it to whoever claims it
    B. keep the purse until someone claims it
    C. immediately deliver the purse to the "lost and found" desk
    D. ask the lady who is nearest to him if she lost a purse

47. Special officers often have the power of arrest.
    Of the following, the BEST reason for this practice is to

    A. have the officer always arrest any person who refuses to obey his orders
    B. aid in maintaining order in places where he is assigned
    C. promote good public relations
    D. aid in preventing illegal use of public buildings by tenants or employees

48. An officer has told a mother that he found her son writing on the walls of the building with chalk. The mother tells the officer that he should be more concerned with "crooks" than with children's minor pranks.
    Of the following, the BEST answer for the officer to make to this woman is that

    A. children should be taught good conduct by their parents
    B. damage to public property means higher taxes
    C. serious criminals often begin their careers with minor violations
    D. it is his duty to enforce all rules and regulations

49. A man asks you, a special officer, where to get a certain kind of license not issued in your office. You don't know where such licenses are issued.
    Of the following, the BEST procedure for you to follow is to

    A. refer him to the manager of the office
    B. get the information if you can and give it to the man
    C. tell the man to inquire at any police station house
    D. tell the man that you just do not know

50. Special officers are not permitted to ask private citizens to buy tickets for dances or other such social functions, not even when such functions are operated by charitable organizations. Of the following, the BEST reason for this rule is that

    A. private citizens are under no obligation to buy any such tickets
    B. not all groups are allowed equal opportunity in the sale of their tickets
    C. private citizens might complain to officials
    D. private citizens might feel they would not get proper service unless they bought such tickets

KEY (CORRECT ANSWERS)

1. B	11. D	21. B	31. A	41. D
2. C	12. B	22. B	32. C	42. B
3. B	13. C	23. D	33. D	43. C
4. D	14. A	24. C	34. C	44. B
5. A	15. A	25. A	35. B	45. A
6. A	16. D	26. B	36. D	46. C
7. C	17. C	27. A	37. D	47. B
8. A	18. C	28. C	38. C	48. D
9. B	19. A	29. B	39. D	49. B
10. A	20. B	30. D	40. B	50. D

SOLUTIONS TO ARITHMETIC PROBLEMS

11. $2\frac{1}{4}$ miles are completed in 1 1/2 minutes (1 minute and 30 seconds)

    $\therefore 2\frac{1}{4} \div 1\frac{1}{2}$ = rate per minute

    $= \frac{9}{4} \div 1\frac{1}{2}$

    $= \frac{9}{4} \div \frac{3}{2}$

    $= \frac{9}{4} \times \frac{2}{3}$

    $= \frac{3}{2}$ miles per minute

    $\therefore \frac{3}{2} \times 60$ (minutes in an hour) = rate per hour = 90 miles per hour

    (Ans. D)

12. 550 + 2230 = 2780; 21,500 - 2780 = 18,720 passengers

550 buses at $14.00	=	$ 7,700
2230 trucks at $7.00	=	15,610
18720 passengers at $3.50	=	65,520
		$88,830

    (Ans. B)

13. Given: speed = 100 feet the first second

100 - 10 (10% of 100)	=	90 feet - the second second
90 - 9 (10% of 90)	=	81 feet - the third second
81 - 8.1 (10% of 81)	=	72.9 feet - the fourth second
		343.9 (total at end of the fourth second)

    (Ans. C)

14. Given: 500 = uniform allowance

$500 - 180	=	$320	(amount left after buying winter jacket)
$320 x 40%	=	$128	(amount spent for two pairs of trousers)
$320 - 128	=	$192	(amount now left)

    Since the winter overcoat costs $240, he is now short $48 ($240 - 192) or 20% of the purchase price of the overcoat. (48/240 = $\frac{1}{5}$ = 20%)

(Ans. A)

15. Light care: 9000(miles)÷30(miles per gallon)×3.75(per gallon)

$$= \frac{9000}{30} \times 3.75$$
$$= 300 \times 3.75$$
$$= \$1,125 \text{ (total gasoline cost)}$$

Standard cars: 9000 (miles) ÷ 15 (miles per gallon) x 3.75

$$= \frac{9000}{15} \times 3.75$$
$$= 600 \times 3.75$$
$$= \$2,250 \text{ (total gasoline cost)}$$

∴ use of light car would result in a saving in gasoline costs of $1,125 ($2,250 - $1,125).

(Ans. A)

16. 2006: 14,200   (burglary)
    2005: 12,800   (burglary)
           1,400   (increase in burglaries)

    2006: 34,750   (felony)
    2005: 32,300   (felony)
           2,450   (increase in felonies

$$\therefore 1400 \div 2450 = \frac{1400}{2450} = .57$$

WORK

```
           .57
    2450)1400.0
         1225.0
          175.00
          171.50
```

(Ans. D)

17. Given: smaller office: grants permits to 40% of 1/3 of the total number of applicants (900)

    larger office: grants permits to 60% of 2/3 of the total number of applicants (900)

    Solving: smaller office: $.40 \times \frac{1}{3} \times 900 = 120$ permits

    larger office: $.60 \times \frac{2}{3} \times 900 = \underline{360}$ permits
    $\phantom{larger office: .60 \times \frac{2}{3} \times 900 =}$ 480 permits (total)

(Ans. C)

EXAMINATION SECTION
TEST 1

DIRECTIONS: Each question or incomplete statement is followed by several suggested answers or completions. Select the one that BEST answers the question or completes the statement. *PRINT THE LETTER OF THE CORRECT ANSWER IN THE SPACE AT THE RIGHT.*

1. Of the following, the MOST important single factor in any building security program is

    A. a fool-proof employee identification system
    B. an effective control of entrances and exits
    C. bright illumination of all outside areas
    D. clearly marking public and non-public areas

    1.____

2. There is general agreement that the BEST criterion of what is a good physical security system in a large public building is

    A. the number of uniformed officers needed to patrol sensitive areas
    B. how successfully the system prevents rather than detects violations
    C. the number of persons caught in the act of committing criminal offenses
    D. how successfully the system succeeds in maintaining good public relations

    2.____

3. Which one of the following statements most correctly expresses the CHIEF reason why women were originally made eligible for appointment to the position of officer?

    A. Certain tasks in security protection can be performed best by assigning women.
    B. More women than men are available to fill many vacancies in this position.
    C. The government wants more women in law enforcement because of their better attendance records.
    D. Women can no longer be barred from any government jobs because of sex.

    3.____

4. The MOST BASIC purpose of patrol by officers is to

    A. eliminate as much as possible the opportunity for successful misconduct
    B. investigate criminal complaints and accident cases
    C. give prompt assistance to employees and citizens in distress or requesting their help
    D. take persons into custody who commit criminal offenses against persons and property

    4.____

5. The highest quality of patrol service is MOST generally obtained by

    A. frequently changing the post assignments of each officer
    B. assigning officers to posts of equal size
    C. assigning problem officers to the least desirable posts
    D. assigning the same officers to the same posts

    5.____

6. The one of the following requirements which is MOST essential to the successful performance of patrol duty by individual officers is their

    A. ability to communicate effectively with higher-level officers
    B. prompt signalling according to a prescribed schedule to insure post coverages at all times

    6.____

C. knowledge of post conditions and post hazards
D. willingness to cover large areas during periods of critical manpower shortages

7. Officers on patrol are constantly warned to be on the alert for suspicious persons, actions, and circumstances.
   With this in mind, a senior officer should emphasize the need for them to

   A. be cautious and suspicious when dealing officially with any civilian regardless of the latter's overt actions or the circumstances surrounding his dealings with the police
   B. keep looking for the unusual persons, actions, and circumstances on their posts and pay less attention to the usual
   C. take aggressive police action immediately against any unusual person or condition detected on their posts, regardless of any other circumstances
   D. become thoroughly familiar with the usual on their posts so as to be better able to detect the unusual

8. Of primary importance in the safeguarding of property from theft is a good central lock and key issuance and control system.
   Which one of the following recommendations about maintaining such a control system would be LEAST acceptable?

   A. In selecting locks to be used for the various gates, building, and storage areas, consideration should be given to the amount of security desired.
   B. Master keys should have no markings that will identify them as such and the list of holders of these keys should be frequently reviewed to determine the continuing necessity for the individuals having them.
   C. Whenever keys for outside doors or gates or for other doors which permit access to important buildings and areas are misplaced, the locks should be immediately changed or replaced pending an investigation.
   D. Whenever an employee fails to return a borrowed key at the time specified, a prompt investigation should be made by the security force.

9. In a crowded building, a fire develops in the basement, and smoke enters the crowded rooms on the first floor. Of the following, the BEST action for an officer to take after an alarm is turned in is to

   A. call out a warning that the building is on fire and that everyone should evacuate because of the immediate danger
   B. call all of the officers together for an emergency meeting and discuss a plan of action
   C. immediately call for assistance from the local police station to help in evacuating the crowd
   D. tell everyone that there is a fire in the building next door and that they should move out onto the streets through available exits

10. Which of the following is in a key position to carry out successfully a safety program of an agency? The

    A. building engineer   B. bureau chiefs
    C. immediate supervisors   D. public relations director

11. It is GENERALLY considered that a daily roll call inspection, which checks to see that the officers and their equipment are in good order, is

    A. *desirable,* chiefly because it informs the superior officer what men will have to purchase new uniforms within a month
    B. *desirable,* chiefly because the public forms their impressions of the organization from the appearance of the officers
    C. *undesirable,* chiefly because this kind of daily inspection unnecessarily delays officers in getting to their assigned patrol posts
    D. *undesirable,* chiefly because roll call inspection usually misses individuals reporting to work late

11.____

12. A supervising officer in giving instructions to a group of officers on the principles of accident investigation remarked, "A conclusion that appears reasonable will often be changed by exploring a factor of apparently little importance".
    Which one of the following precautions does this statement emphasize as MOST important in any accident investigation?

    A. Every accident clue should be fully investigated.
    B. Accidents should not be too promptly investigated.
    C. Only specially trained officers should investigate accidents.
    D. Conclusions about accident causes are highly unreliable.

12.____

13. On a rainy day, a senior officer found that 9 of his 50 officers reported to work. What percentage of his officers was ABSENT?

    A. 18%   B. 80%   C. 82%   D. 90%

13.____

14. Officer A and Officer B work at the same post on the same days, but their hours are different. Officer A comes to work at 9:00 A.M. and leaves at 5:00 P.M., with a lunch period between 12:15 P.M. and 1:15 P.M. Officer B comes to work at 10:50 A.M. and works until 6:50 P.M., and he takes an hour for lunch between 3:00 P.M. and 4:00 P.M. What is the total amount of time between 9:00 A.M. and 6:50 P.M. that only ONE officer will be on duty?

    A. 4 hours
    C. 5 hours
    B. 4 hours and 40 minutes
    D. 5 hours and 40 minutes

14.____

15. An officer's log recorded the following attendance of 30 officers:

Day	Present	Absent
Monday	20 present;	10 absent
Tuesday	28 present;	2 absent
Wednesday	30 present;	0 absent
Thursday	21 present;	9 absent
Friday	16 present;	14 absent
Saturday	11 present;	19 absent
Sunday	14 present;	16 absent

    On the average, how many men were present on the weekdays (Monday - Friday)?

    A. 21   B. 23   C. 25   D. 27

15.____

16. An angry woman is being questioned by an officer when she begins shouting abuses at him.
The BEST of the following procedures for the officer to follow is to

    A. leave the room until she has cooled off
    B. politely ignore anything she says
    C. place her under arrest by handcuffing her to a fixed object
    D. warn her that he will have to use force to restrain her making remarks

17. Of the following, which is NOT a recommended practice for an officer placing a woman offender under arrest?

    A. Assume that the offender is an innocent and virtuous person and treat her accordingly.
    B. Protect himself from attack by the woman.
    C. Refrain from using excessive physical force on the offender.
    D. Make the public aware that he is not abusing the woman.

Questions 18-21.

DIRECTIONS: Questions 18 through 21 are to be answered SOLELY on the basis of the following passage.

Specific measures for prevention of pilferage will be based on careful analysis of the conditions at each agency. The most practical and effective method to control casual pilferage is the establishment of psychological deterrents.

One of the most common means of discouraging casual pilferage is to search individuals leaving the agency at unannounced times and places. These spot searches may occasionally detect attempts at theft but greater value is realized by bringing to the attention of individuals the fact that they may be apprehended if they do attempt the illegal removal of property.

An aggressive security education program is an effective means of convincing employees that they have much more to lose than they do to gain by engaging in acts of theft. It is important for all employees to realize that pilferage is morally wrong no matter how insignificant the value of the item which is taken. In establishing any deterrent to casual pilferage, security officers must not lose sight of the fact that most employees are honest and disapprove of thievery. Mutual respect between security personnel and other employees of the agency must be maintained if the facility is to be protected from other more dangerous forms of human hazards. Any security measure which infringes on the human rights or dignity of others will jeopardize, rather than enhance, the overall protection of the agency.

18. The $100,000 yearly inventory of an agency revealed that $50 worth of goods had been stolen; the only individuals with access to the stolen materials were the employees. Of the following measures, which would the author of the preceding paragraph MOST likely recommend to a security officer?

    A. Conduct an intensive investigation of all employees to find the culprit.
    B. Make a record of the theft, but take no investigative or disciplinary action against any employee.
    C. Place a tight security check on all future movements of personnel.
    D. Remove the remainder of the material to an area with much greater security.

19. What does the passage imply is the percentage of employees whom a security officer should expect to be honest? 19.____

    A. No employee can be expected to be honest all of the time
    B. Just 50%
    C. Less than 50%
    D. More than 50%

20. According to the passage, the security officer would use which of the following methods to minimize theft in buildings with many exits when his staff is very small? 20.____

    A. Conduct an inventory of all material and place a guard near that which is most likely to be pilfered.
    B. Inform employees of the consequences of legal prosecution for pilfering.
    C. Close off the unimportant exits and have all his men concentrate on a few exits.
    D. Place a guard at each exit and conduct a casual search of individuals leaving the premises.

21. Of the following, the title BEST suited for this passage is: 21.____

    A. Control Measures for Casual Pilfering
    B. Detecting the Potential Pilferer
    C. Financial losses Resulting from Pilfering
    D. The Use of Moral Persuasion in Physical Security

22. Of the following first aid procedures, which will cause the GREATEST harm in treating a fracture? 22.____

    A. Control hemorrhages by applying direct pressure
    B. Keep the broken portion from moving about
    C. Reset a protruding bone by pressing it back into place
    D. Treat the suffering person for shock

23. During a snowstorm, a man comes to you complaining of frostbitten hands. PROPER first aid treatment in this case is to 23.____

    A. place the hands under hot running water
    B. place the hands in lukewarm water
    C. call a hospital and wait for medical aid
    D. rub the hands in melting snow

24. While on duty, an officer sees a woman apparently in a state of shock. Of the following, which one is NOT a symptom of shock? 24.____

    A. Eyes lacking luster
    B. A cold, moist forehead
    C. A shallow, irregular breathing
    D. A strong, throbbing pulse

25. You notice a man entering your building who begins coughing violently, has shortness of breath, and complains of severe chest pains. These symptoms are GENERALLY indicative of 25.____

    A. a heart attack   B. a stroke
    C. internal bleeding   D. an epileptic seizure

26. When an officer is required to record the rolled fingerprint impressions of a prisoner on the standard fingerprint form, the technique recommended by the F.B.I, as MOST likely to result in obtaining clear impressions is to roll

    A. all fingers away from the center of the prisoner's body
    B. all fingers toward the center of the prisoner's body
    C. the thumbs away from and the other fingers toward the center of the prisoner's body
    D. the thumbs toward and the other fingers away from the center of the prisoner's body

27. The principle which underlies the operation and use of a lie detector machine is that

    A. a person who is not telling the truth will be able to give a consistent story
    B. a guilty mind will unconsciously associate ideas in a very indicative manner
    C. the presence of emotional stress in a person will result in certain abnormal physical reactions
    D. many individuals are not afraid to lie

Questions 28-32.

DIRECTIONS: Questions 28 through 32 are based SOLELY on the following diagram and the paragraph preceding this group of questions. The paragraph will be divided into two statements. Statement one (1) consists of information given to the senior officer by an agency director; *this information will detail the specific security objectives the senior officer has to meet.* Statement two (2) gives the resources available to the senior officer.

NOTE: The questions are correctly answered only when all of the agency's objectives have been met and when the officer has used all his resources efficiently (i.e., to their maximum effectiveness) in meeting these objectives. All X's in the diagram indicate possible locations of officers' posts. Each X has a corresponding number which is to be used when referring to that location.

DIAGRAM

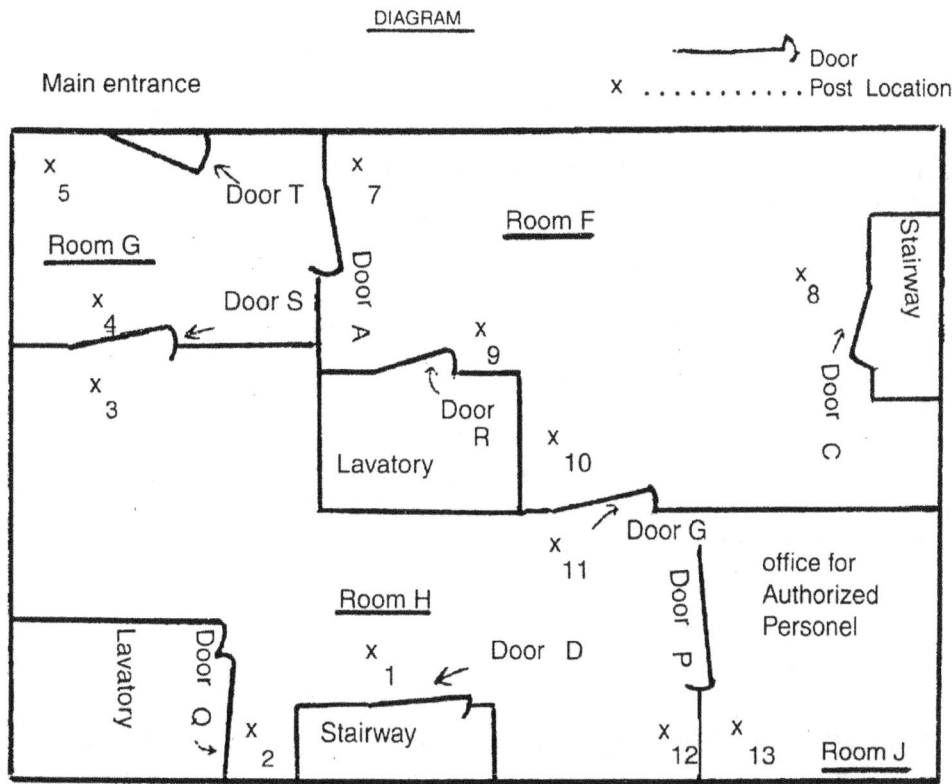

PARAGRAPH

PARAGRAPH

STATEMENT 1: Room G will be the public intake room from which persons will be directed to Room F or Room H; under no circumstances are they to enter the wrong room, and they are not to move from Room F to Room H or vice-versa. A minimum of two officers must be in each room frequented by the public at all times, and they are to keep unauthorized individuals from going to the second floor or into restricted areas. All usable entrances or exits must be covered.

STATEMENT 2: The senior officer can lock any door except the main entrance and stairway doors. He has a staff of five officers to carry out these operations.

NOTE: The senior officer is available for guard duty. Room J is an active office.

28. According to the instructions, how many officers should be assigned inside the office for authorized personnel (Room J)?

    A. 0   B. 1   C. 2   D. 3

28.____

29. In order to keep the public from moving between Room F and Room H, which door(s) can be locked without interfering with normal office operations? Door

    A. G   B. P   C. R and Q   D. S

29.____

30. When placing officers in Room H, the only way the senior officer can satisfy the agency's objectives and his manpower limitations is by placing men at locations

    A. 1 and 3   B. 1 and 12   C. 3 and 11   D. 11 and 12

31. In accordance with the instructions, the LEAST effective locations to place officers in Room F are locations

    A. 7 and 9   B. 7 and 10   C. 8 and 9   D. 9 and 10

32. In which room is it MOST difficult for each of the officers to see all the movements of the public? Room

    A. G   B. F   C. H   D. J

33. According to its own provisions, the Penal Law of the State has a number of general purposes.
    It would be LEAST accurate to state that one of these general purposes is to

    A. give fair warning of the nature of the conduct forbidden and the penalties authorized upon conviction
    B. define the act or omission and accompanying mental state which constitute each offense
    C. regulate the procedure which governs the arrest, trial and punishment of convicted offenders
    D. insure the public safety by preventing the commission of offenses through the deterrent influence of the sentences authorized upon conviction

34. Officers must be well-informed about the meaning of certain terms in connection with their enforcement duties. Which one of the following statements about such terms would be MOST accurate according to the Penal Law of the State? A(n)

    A. offense is always a crime
    B. offense is always a violation
    C. violation is never a crime
    D. felony is never an offense

35. According to the Penal Law of the State, the one of the following elements which must ALWAYS be present in order to justify the arrest of a person for criminal assault is

    A. the infliction of an actual physical injury
    B. an intent to cause an injury
    C. a threat to inflict a physical injury
    D. the use of some kind of weapon

36. A recent law of the State defines who are police officers and who are peace officers. The official title of this law is: The

    A. Criminal Code of Procedure
    B. Law of Criminal Procedure
    C. Criminal Procedure Law
    D. Code of Criminal Procedure

37. If you are required to appear in court to testify as the complainant in a criminal action, it would be MOST important for you to

    A. confine your answers to the questions asked when you are testifying
    B. help the prosecutor even if some exaggeration in your testimony may be necessary
    C. be as fair as possible to the defendant even if some details have to be omitted from your testimony
    D. avoid contradicting other witnesses testifying against the defendant

38. A senior officer is asked by the television news media to explain to the public what happened on his post during an important incident.
    When speaking with departmental permission in front of the tape recorders and cameras, the senior officer can give the MOST favorable impression of himself and his department by

    A. refusing to answer any questions but remaining calm in front of the cameras
    B. giving a detailed report of the wrong decisions made by his agency for handling the particular incident
    C. presenting the appropriate factual information in a competent way
    D. telling what should have been done during the incident and how such incidents will be handled in the future

39. Of the following suggested guidelines for officers, the one which is LEAST likely to be effective in promoting good manners and courtesy in their daily contacts with the public is:

    A. Treat inquiries by telephone in the same manner as those made in person
    B. Never look into the face of the person to whom you are speaking
    C. Never give misinformation in answer to any inquiry on a matter on which you are uncertain of the facts
    D. Show respect and consideration in both trivial and important contacts with the public

40. Assume you are an officer who has had a record of submitting late weekly reports and that you are given an order by your supervisor which is addressed to all line officers. The order states that weekly reports will be replaced by twice-weekly reports.
    The MOST logical conclusion for you to make, of the following, is:

    A. Fully detailed information was missing from your past reports
    B. Most officers have submitted late reports
    C. The supervisor needs more timely information
    D. The supervisor is attempting to punish you for your past late reports

41. A young man with long hair and "mod" clothing makes a complaint to an officer about the rudeness of another officer.
    If the senior officer is not on the premises, the officer receiving the complaint should

    A. consult with the officer who is being accused to see if the youth's story is true
    B. refer the young man to central headquarters
    C. record the complaint made against his fellow officer and ask the youth to wait until he can locate the senior officer
    D. search for the senior officer and bring him back to the site of the complainant

42. During a demonstration, which area should ALWAYS be kept clear of demonstrators? 42.___

   A. Water fountains
   B. Seating areas
   C. Doorways
   D. Restrooms

43. During demonstrations, an officer's MOST important duty is to 43.___

   A. aid the agency's employees to perform their duties
   B. promptly arrest those who might cause incidents
   C. promptly disperse the crowds of demonstrators
   D. keep the demonstrators from disrupting order

44. Of the following, what is the FIRST action a senior officer should take if a demonstration develops in his area without advance warning? 44.___

   A. Call for additional assistance from the police department
   B. Find the leaders of the demonstrators and discuss their demands
   C. See if the demonstrators intend to break the law
   D. Inform his superiors of the event taking place

45. If a senior officer is informed in the morning that a demonstration will take place during the afternoon at his assigned location, he should assemble his officers to discuss the nature and aspects of this demonstration. Of the following, the subject which it is LEAST important to discuss during this meeting is 45.___

   A. making a good impression if an officer is called before the television cameras for a personal interview
   B. the known facts and causes of the demonstration
   C. the attitude and expected behavior of the demonstrators
   D. the individual responsibilities of the officers during the demonstration

46. A male officer has probable reason to believe that a group of women occupying the ladies' toilet are using illicit drugs.
The BEST action, of the following, for the officer to take is to 46.___

   A. call for assistance and, with the aid of such assistance, enter the toilet and escort the occupants outside
   B. ignore the situation but recommend that the ladies' toilet be closed temporarily
   C. immediately rush into the ladies' toilet and search the occupants therein
   D. knock on the door of the ladies' toilet and ask their permission to enter so that he will not be accused of trying to molest them

47. Assume that you know that a group of demonstrators will not cooperate with your request to throw handbills in a waste basket instead of on the sidewalk. You ask one of the leaders of the group, who agrees with you, to speak to the demonstrators and ask for their cooperation in this matter.
Your request of the group leader is 47.___

   A. *desirable,* chiefly because an officer needs civilians to control the public since the officer is usually unfriendly to the views of public groups
   B. *undesirable,* chiefly because an officer should never request a civilian to perform his duties
   C. *desirable,* chiefly because the appeal of an acknowledged leader helps in gaining group cooperation

D. *undesirable*, chiefly because an institutional leader is motivated to maneuver a situation to gain his own personal advantage

48. A vague letter received from a female employee in the agency accuses an officer of improper conduct.
The initial investigative interview by the senior officer assigned to check the accusation should GENERALLY be with the

   A. accused officer
   B. female employee
   C. highest superior about disciplinary action against the officer
   D. immediate supervisor of the female employee

Questions 49-50.

DIRECTIONS: Questions 49 and 50 are to be answered SOLELY on the basis of the information in the following paragraph.

The personal conduct of each member of the Department is the primary factor in promoting desirable police-community relations. Tact, patience, and courtesy shall be strictly observed under all circumstances. A favorable public attitude toward the police must be earned; it is influenced by the personal conduct and attitude of each member of the force, by his personal integrity and courteous manner, by his respect for due process of law, by his devotion to the principles of justice, fairness, and impartiality.

49. According to the preceding paragraph, what is the BEST action an officer can take in dealing with people in a neighborhood?

   A. Assist neighborhood residents by doing favors for them.
   B. Give special attention to the community leaders in order to be able to control them effectively.
   C. Behave in an appropriate manner and give all community members the same just treatment.
   D. Prepare a plan detailing what he, the officer, wants to do for the community and submit it for approval.

50. As used in the paragraph, the word *impartiality* means *most nearly*

   A. observant   B. unbiased
   C. righteousness   D. honesty

KEY (CORRECT ANSWERS)

1. B	11. B	21. A	31. D	41. C
2. B	12. A	22. C	32. C	42. C
3. A	13. C	23. B	33. C	43. D
4. A	14. D	24. D	34. C	44. D
5. D	15. B	25. A	35. A	45. A
6. C	16. B	26. D	36. C	46. A
7. D	17. A	27. C	37. A	47. C
8. C	18. B	28. A	38. C	48. B
9. D	19. D	29. A	39. B	49. C
10. C	20. B	30. B	40. C	50. B

TEST 2

DIRECTIONS: Each question or incomplete statement is followed by several suggested answers or completions. Select the one that BEST answers the question or completes the statement. *PRINT THE LETTER OF THE CORRECT ANSWER IN THE SPACE AT THE RIGHT.*

Questions 1-5.

DIRECTIONS: Questions 1 through 5 consist of short paragraphs. Each paragraph contains one word which is INCORRECTLY used because it is NOT in keeping with the meaning of the paragraph. Find the word in each paragraph which is INCORRECTLY used, and then select as the answer the suggested word which should be substituted for the incorrectly used word.

SAMPLE QUESTION

In determining who is to do the work in your unit, you will have to decide just who does what from day to day. One of your lowest responsibilities is to assign work so that everybody gets a fair share and that everyone can do his part well.
    A. new   B. old   C. important   D. performance

EXPLANATION

The word which is NOT in keeping with the meaning of the paragraph is "lowest". This is the INCORRECTLY used word. The suggested word "important" would be in keeping with the meaning of the paragraph and should be substituted for "lowest". Therefore, the CORRECT answer is Choice C.

1. If really good practice in the elimination of preventable injuries is to be achieved and held in any establishment, top management must refuse full and definite responsibility and must apply a good share of its attention to the task.

    A. accept   B. avoidable   C. duties   D. problem

2. Recording the human face for identification is by no means the only service performed by the camera in the field of investigation. When the trial of any issue takes place, a word picture is sought to be distorted to the court of incidents, occurrences, or events which are in dispute.

    A. appeals   B. description
    C. portrayed   D. deranged

3. In the collection of physical evidence, it cannot be emphasized too strongly that a haphazard systematic search at the scene of the crime is vital. Nothing must be overlooked. Often the only leads in a case will come from the results of this search.

    A. important   B. investigation
    C. proof   D. thorough

4. If an investigator has reason to suspect that the witness is mentally stable or a habitual drunkard, he should leave no stone unturned in his investigation to determine if the witness was under the influence of liquor or drugs, or was mentally unbalanced either at the time of the occurrence to which he testified or at the time of the trial.

    A. accused   B. clue   C. deranged   D. question

5. The use of records is a valuable step in crime investigation and is the main reason every department should maintain accurate reports. Crimes are not committed through the use of departmental records alone but from the use of all records, of almost every type, wherever they may be found and whenever they give any incidental information regarding the criminal.

   A. accidental   B. necessary   C. reported   D. solved

Questions 6-8.

DIRECTIONS: Questions 6 through 8 are to be answered SOLELY on the basis of the following passage.

The mass media are an integral part of the daily life of virtually every American. Among these media, the youngest, television, is the most persuasive. Ninety-five percent of American homes have at least one television set, and on the average that set is in use for about 40 hours each week. The central place of television in American life makes this medium the focal point of a growing national concern over the effects of media portrayals of violence on the values, attitudes, and behavior of an ever increasing audience.

In our concern about violence and its causes, it is easy to make television a scapegoat. But we emphasise the fact that there is no simple answer to the problem of violence -- no single explanation of its causes, and no single prescription for its control. It should be remembered that America also experienced high levels of crime and violence in periods before the advent of television.

The problem of balance, taste, and artistic merit in entertaining programs on television are complex. We cannot countenance government censorship of television. Nor would we seek to impose arbitrary limitations on programming which might jeopardize television's ability to deal in dramatic presentations with controversial social issues. Nonetheless, we are deeply troubled by television's constant portrayal of violence, not in any genuine attempt to focus artistic expression on the human condition, but rather in pandering to a public preoccupation with violence that television itself has helped to generate.

6. According to the passage, television uses violence MAINLY

   A. to highlight the reality of everyday existence
   B. to satisfy the audience's hunger for destructive action
   C. to shape the values and attitudes of the public
   D. when it films documentaries concerning human conflict

7. Which one of the following statements is BEST supported by this passage?

   A. Early American history reveals a crime pattern which is not related to television.
   B. Programs should give presentations of social issues and never portray violent acts.
   C. Television has proven that entertainment programs can easily make the balance between taste and artistic merit a simple matter.
   D. Values and behavior should be regulated by governmental censorship.

8. Of the following, which word has the same meaning as countenance as it is used in the above passage?

   A. approve   B. exhibit   C. oppose   D. reject

Questions 9-12.

DIRECTIONS: Questions 9 through 12 are to be answered SOLELY on the basis of the following graph relating to the burglary rate in the city, 2003 to 2008, inclusive.

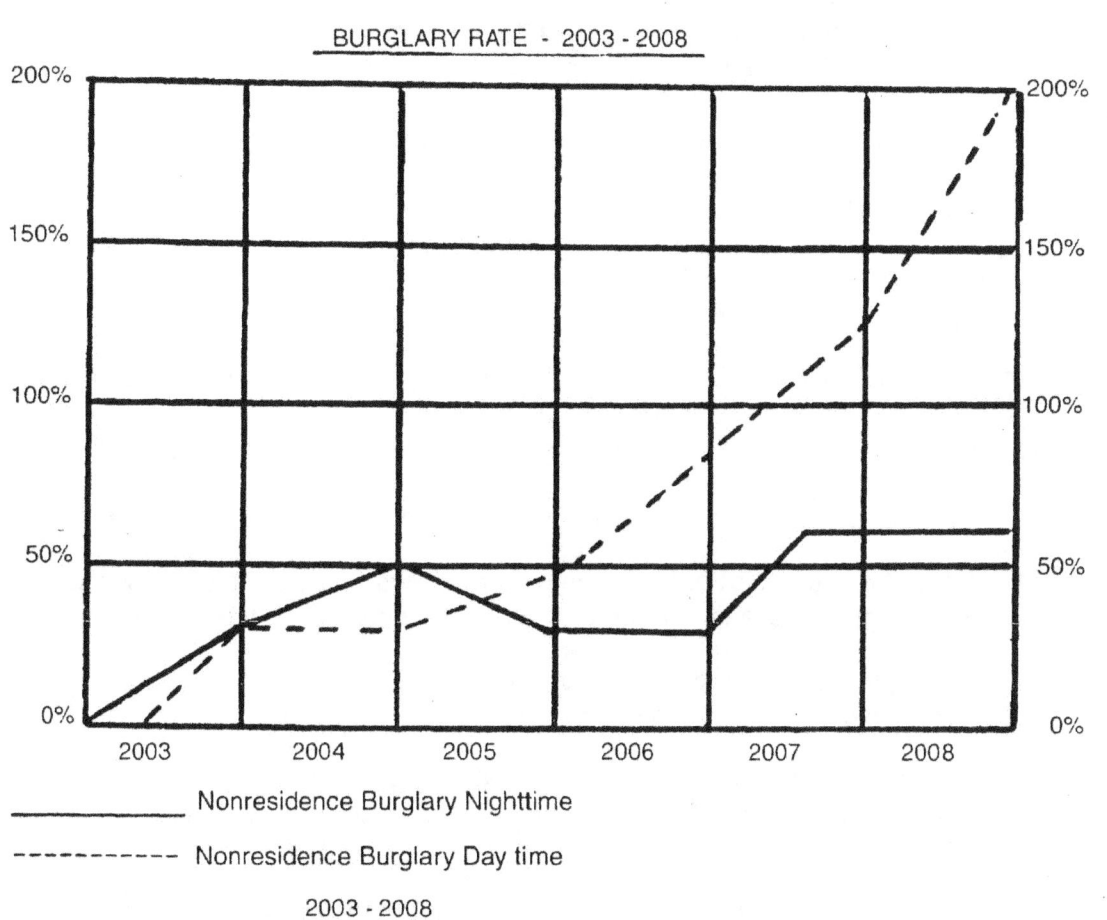

2003 - 2008

9. At the beginning of what year was the percentage increase in daytime and nighttime burglaries the SAME?

    A. 2004   B. 2005   C. 2006   D. 2008

10. In what year did the percentage of nighttime burglaries DECREASE?

    A. 2003   B. 2005   C. 2006   D. 2008

11. In what year was there the MOST rapid increase in the percentage of daytime non-residence burglaries?

    A. 2004   B. 2006   C. 2007   D. 2008

12. At the end of 2007, the actual number of nighttime burglaries committed

    A. was about 20%
    B. was 40%
    C. was 400
    D. cannot be determined from the information given

Questions 13-17.

DIRECTIONS: Questions 13 through 17 consist of two sentences numbered 1 and 2 taken from police officers' reports. Some of these sentences are correct according to ordinary formal English usage. Other sentences are incorrect because they contain errors in English usage or punctuation. Consider a sentence correct if it contains no errors in English usage or punctuation even if there may be other ways of writing the sentence correctly. Mark your answer to each question in the space at the right as follows:
- A. If only sentence 1 is correct, but not sentence 2
- B. If only sentence 2 is correct, but not sentence 1
- C. If sentences 1 and 2 are both correct
- D. If sentences 1 and 2 are both incorrect

SAMPLE QUESTION
1. The woman claimed that the purse was her's.
2. Everyone of the new officers was assigned to a patrol post.

EXPLANATION

Sentence 1 is INCORRECT because of an error in punctuation. The possessive words, "ours, yours, hers, theirs," do not have the apostrophe (').

Sentence 2 is CORRECT because the subject of the sentence is "Everyone" which is singular and requires the singular verb "was assigned".

Since only sentence 2 is correct, but not sentence 1, the CORRECT answer is B.

13. 1. Either the patrolman or his sergeant are always ready to help the public.   13.___
    2. The sergeant asked the patrolman when he would finish the report.

14. 1. The injured man could not hardly talk.   14.___
    2. Every officer had ought to hand in their reports on time.

15. 1. Approaching the victim of the assault, two large bruises were noticed by me.   15.___
    2. The prisoner was arrested for assault, resisting arrest, and use of a deadly weapon.

16. 1. A copy of the orders, which had been prepared by the captain, was given to each patrolman.   16.___
    2. It's always necessary to inform an arrested person of his constitutional rights before asking him any questions.

17. 1. To prevent further bleeding, I applied a tourniquet tothe wound.   17.___
    2. John Rano a senior officer was on duty at the time of the accident.

Questions 18-25.

DIRECTIONS: Answer each of Questions 18 through 25 SOLELY on the basis of the statement preceding the questions.

18. The criminal is one whose habits have been erroneously developed or, we should say,   18.___
developed in anti-social patterns, and therefore the task of dealing with him is not one of punishment, but of treatment.
The basic principle expressed in this statement is BEST illustrated by the

- A. emphasis upon rehabilitation in penal institutions
- B. prevalence of capital punishment for murder
- C. practice of imposing heavy fines for minor violations
- D. legal provision for trial by jury in criminal cases

19. The writ of habeas corpus is one of the great guarantees of personal liberty. Of the following, the BEST justification for this statement is that the writ of habeas corpus is frequently used to

   A. compel the appearance in court of witnesses who are outside the state
   B. obtain the production of books and records at a criminal trial
   C. secure the release of a person improperly held in custody
   D. prevent the use of deception in obtaining testimony of reluctant witnesses

19._____

20. Fifteen persons suffered effects of carbon dioxide asphyxiation shortly before noon recently in a seventh-floor pressing shop. The accident occurred in a closed room where six steam presses were in operation. Four men and one woman were overcome.
Of the following, the MOST probable reason for the fact that so many people were affected simultaneously is that

   A. women evidently show more resistance to the effects of carbon dioxide than men
   B. carbon dioxide is an odorless and colorless gas
   C. carbon dioxide is lighter than air
   D. carbon dioxide works more quickly at higher altitudes

20._____

21. Lay the patient on his stomach, one arm extended directly overhead, the other arm bent at the elbow, and with the face turned outward and resting on hand or forearm.
To the officer who is skilled at administering first aid, these instructions should IMMEDIATELY suggest

   A. application of artificial respiration
   B. treatment for third degree burns of the arm
   C. setting a dislocated shoulder
   D. control of capillary bleeding in the stomach

21._____

22. The soda and acid fire extinguisher is the hand extinguisher most commonly used by officers. The main body of the cylinder is filled with a mixture of water and bicarbonate of soda. In a separate interior compartment, at the top, is a small bottle of sulphuric acid. When the extinguisher is inverted, the acid spills into the solution below and starts a chemical reaction. The carbon dioxide thereby generated forces the solution from the extinguisher.
The officer who understands the operation of this fire extinguisher should know that it is LEAST likely to operate properly

   A. in basements or cellars
   B. in extremely cold weather
   C. when the reaction is of a chemical nature
   D. when the bicarbonate of soda is in solution

22._____

23. Suppose that, at a training lecture, you are told that many of the men in our penal institutions today are second and third offenders.
Of the following, the MOST valid inference you can make SOLELY on the basis of this statement is that

   A. second offenders are not easily apprehended
   B. patterns of human behavior are not easily changed
   C. modern laws are not sufficiently flexible
   D. laws do not breed crimes

23._____

24. In all societies of our level of culture, acts are committed which arouse censure severe enough to take the form of punishment by the government. Such acts are crimes, not because of their inherent nature, but because of their ability to arouse resentment and to stimulate repressive measures.
Of the following, the MOST valid inference which can be drawn from this statement is that

   A. society unjustly punishes acts which are inherently criminal
   B. many acts are not crimes but are punished by society because such acts threaten the lives of innocent people
   C. only modern society has a level of culture
   D. societies sometimes disagree as to what acts are crimes

25. Crime cannot be measured directly. Its amount must be inferred from the frequency of some occurrence connected with it; for example, crimes brought to the attention of the police, persons arrested, prosecutions, convictions, and other dispositions, such as probation or commitment. Each of these may be used as an index of the amount of crime.
SOLELY on the basis of the foregoing statement, it is MOST correct to state that

   A. the incidence of crime cannot be estimated with any accuracy
   B. the number of commitments is usually greater than the number of probationary sentences
   C. the amount of crime is ordinarily directly correlated with the number of persons arrested
   D. a joint consideration of crimes brought to the attention of the police and the number of prosecutions undertaken gives little indication of the amount of crime in a locality

KEY (CORRECT ANSWERS)

1.	B	11.	D
2.	A	12.	D
3.	D	13.	D
4.	C	14.	D
5.	D	15.	B
6.	B	16.	C
7.	A	17.	A
8.	A	18.	A
9.	A	19.	C
10.	B	20.	B

21. A
22. B
23. B
24. D
25. C

EXAMINATION SECTION
TEST 1

DIRECTIONS: Each question or incomplete statement is followed by several suggested answers or completions. Select the one that BEST answers the question or completes the statement. *PRINT THE LETTER OF THE CORRECT ANSWER IN THE SPACE AT THE RIGHT.*

Questions 1-4.

DIRECTIONS: Questions 1 through 4 are based on the picture entitled *Contents of a Woman's Handbag*. Assume that all of the contents are shown in the picture.

CONTENTS OF A WOMAN'S HANDBAG

1. Where does Gladys Constantine live?

    A. Chalmers Street in Manhattan
    B. Summer Street in Manhattan
    C. Summer Street in Brooklyn
    D. Chalmers Street in Brooklyn

2. How many keys were in the handbag?

    A. 2   B. 3   C. 4   D. 5

3. How much money was in the handbag? _____ dollar(s).

    A. Exactly five   B. More than five
    C. Exactly ten   D. Less than one

4. The sales slip found in the handbag shows the purchase of which of the following?

    A. The handbag   B. Lipstick
    C. Tissues   D. Prescription medicine

Questions 5-8.

DIRECTIONS: Questions 5 through 8 are based on the floor plan below.

FLOOR PLAN

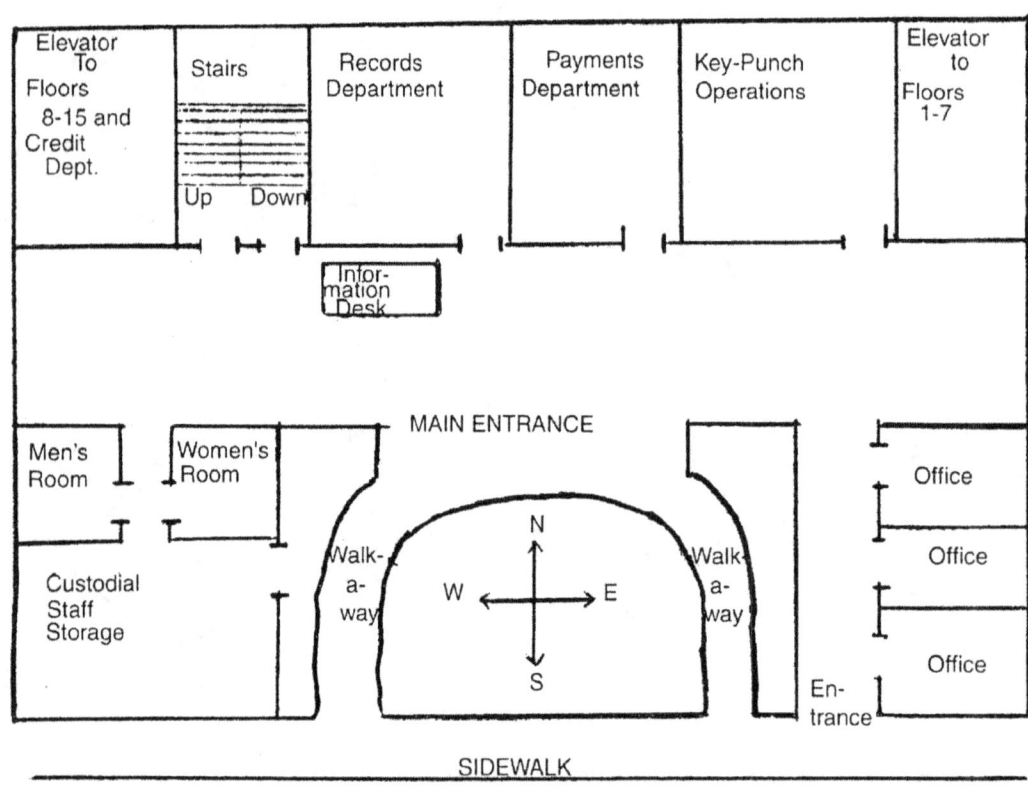

5. A special officer (security officer) on duty at the main entrance must be aware of other outside entrances to his area of the building. These unguarded entrances are usually kept locked, but they are important in case of fire or other emergency.
   Besides the main entrance, how many OTHER entrances shown on the floor plan directly face Forty-ninth Street?
   _____ other entrances.

   A. No   B. One   C. Two   D. Three

6. A person who arrives at the main entrance and asks to be directed to the Credit Department SHOULD be told to

   A. take the elevator on the left
   B. take the elevator on the right
   C. go to a different entrance
   D. go up the stairs on the left

7. On the east side of the entrance can be found

   A. a storage room   B. offices
   C. toilets   D. stairs

8. The space DIRECTLY BEHIND the Information Desk in the floor plan is occupied by

   A. up and down stairs   B. key punch operations
   C. toilets   D. the records department

Questions 9-12.

DIRECTIONS: Answer Questions 9 to 12 on the basis of the information given in the passage below.

The public often believes that the main job of a uniformed officer is to enforce laws by simply arresting people. In reality, however, many of the situations that an officer deals with do not call for the use of his arrest power. In the first place, an officer spends much of his time <u>preventing</u> crimes from happening, by spotting potential violations or suspicious behavior and taking action to prevent illegal acts. In the second place, many of the situations in which officers are called on for assistance involve elements like personal arguments, husband-wife quarrels, noisy juveniles, or mentally disturbed persons. The majority of these problems do not result in arrests and convictions, and often they do not even involve illegal behavior. In the third place, even in situations where there seems to be good reason to make an arrest, an officer may have to exercise very good judgment. There are times when making an arrest too soon could touch off a riot, or could result in the detention of a minor offender while major offenders escaped, or could cut short the gathering of necessary on-the-scene evidence.

9. The above passage IMPLIES that most citizens

   A. will start to riot if they see an arrest being made
   B. appreciate the work that law enforcement officers do
   C. do not realize that making arrests is only a small part of law enforcement
   D. never call for assistance unless they are involved in a personal argument or a husband-wife quarrel

10. According to the passage, one way in which law enforcement officers can prevent crimes from happening is by

    A. arresting suspicious characters
    B. letting minor offenders go free
    C. taking action on potential violations
    D. refusing to get involved in husband-wife fights

11. According to the passage, which of the following statements is NOT true of situations involving mentally disturbed persons?

    A. It is a waste of time to call on law enforcement officers for assistance in such situations.
    B. Such situations may not involve illegal behavior
    C. Such situations often do not result in arrests.
    D. Citizens often turn to law enforcement officers for help in such situations.

12. The last sentence in the passage mentions *detention of minor offenders.*
    Of the following, which BEST explains the meaning of the word *detention* as used here?

    A. Sentencing someone
    B. Indicting someone
    C. Calling someone before a grand jury
    D. Arresting someone

Questions 13-28.

DIRECTIONS: In answering Questions 13 through 28, assume that *you* means a special officer (security officer) on duty. Your basic responsibilities are safeguarding people and property and maintaining order in the area to which you are assigned. You are in uniform, and you are not armed. You keep in touch with your supervisory station either by telephone or by a two-way radio (walkie-talkie).

13. It is a general rule that if the security alarm goes off showing that someone has made an unlawful entrance into a building, no officer responsible for security shall proceed to investigate alone. Each officer must be accompanied by at least one other officer.
    Of the following, which is the MOST probable reason for this rule?

    A. It is dangerous for an officer to investigate such a situation alone.
    B. The intruder might try to bribe an officer to let him go.
    C. One officer may be inexperienced and needs an experienced partner.
    D. Two officers are better than one officer in writing a report of the investigation.

14. You are on weekend duty on the main floor of a public building. The building is closed to the public on weekends, but some employees are sometimes asked to work weekends. You have been instructed to use cautious good judgment in opening the door for such persons.
    Of the following, which one MOST clearly shows the poorest judgment?

A. Admitting an employee who is personally known to you without asking to see any identification except the permit slip signed by the employee's supervisor
B. Refusing to admit someone whom you do not recognize but who claims left his identification at home
C. Admitting to the building only those who can give a detailed description of their weekend work duties
D. Leaving the entrance door locked for a while to make regulation security checks of other areas in the building with the result that no one can either enter or leave during these periods

15. You are on duty at a public building. An office employee tells you that she left her purse in her desk when she went out to lunch, and she has just discovered that it is gone. She has been back from lunch for half an hour and has not left her desk during this period. What should you do FIRST?

    A. Warn all security personnel to stop any suspicious-looking person who is seen with a purse
    B. Ask for a description of the purse
    C. Call the Lost and Found and ask if a purse has been turned in
    D. Obtain statements from any employees who were in the office during the lunch hour

16. You are patrolling your assigned area in a public building. You hear a sudden crash and the sound of running footsteps. You investigate and find that someone has forced open a locked entrance to the building. What is the FIRST thing you should do?

    A. Close the door and try to fix the lock so that no one else can get in
    B. Use your two-way radio to report the emergency and summon help
    C. Chase after the person whose running footsteps you heard
    D. Go immediately to your base office and make out a brief written report

17. You and another special officer (security officer) are on duty in the main waiting area at a welfare center. A caseworker calls both of you over and whispers that one of the clients, Richard Roe, may be carrying a gun. Of the following, what is the BEST action for both of you to take?

    A. You should approach the man, one on each side, and one of you should say loudly and clearly, *"Richard Roe, you are under arrest."*
    B. Both of you should ask the man to go with you to a private room, and then find out if he is carrying a gun
    C. Both of you should grab him, handcuff him, and take him to the nearest precinct station house
    D. Both of you should watch him carefully but not do anything unless he actually pulls a gun

18. You are on duty at a welfare center. You are told that a caseworker is being threatened by a man with a knife. You go immediately to the scene, and you find the caseworker lying on the floor with blood spurting from a wound in his arm. You do not know who the attacker is. What should you do FIRST?

    A. Ask the caseworker for a description of the attacker so that you can set out in pursuit and try to catch him
    B. Take down the names and addresses of any witnesses to the incident

C. Give first aid to the caseworker, if you can, and immediately call for an ambulance
D. Search the people standing around in the room for the knife

19. As a special officer (security officer), you have been patrolling a special section of a hospital building for a week. Smoking is not allowed in this section because the oxygen tanks in use here could easily explode. However, you have observed that some employees sneak into the linen-supply room in this section in order to smoke without anybody seeing them.
Of the following, which is the BEST way for you to deal with this situation?

    A. Whenever you catch anyone smoking, call his supervisor immediately
    B. Request the Building Superintendent to put a padlock on the door of the linen-supply room
    C. Ignore the smoking because you do not want to get a reputation for interfering in the private affairs of other employees
    D. Report the situation to your supervisor and follow his instructions

20. You are on duty at a hospital. You have been assigned to guard the main door, and you are responsible for remaining at your post until relieved. On one of the wards for which you are not responsible, there is a patient who was wounded in a street fight. This patient is under arrest for killing another man in this fight, and he is supposed to be under round-the-clock police guard. A nurse tells you that one of the police officers assigned to guard the patient has suddenly taken ill and has to periodically leave his post to go to the washroom. The nurse is worried because she thinks the patient might try to escape.
Of the following, which is the BEST action for you to take?

    A. Tell the nurse to call you whenever the police officer leaves his post so that you can keep an eye on the patient while the officer is gone
    B. Assume that the police officer probably knows his job, and that there is no reason for you to worry
    C. Alert your supervisor to the nurse's report
    D. Warn the police officer that the nurse has been talking about him

21. You are on night duty at a hospital where you are responsible for patrolling a large section of the main building. Your supervisor tells you that there have been several nighttime thefts from a supply room in your section and asks you to be especially alert for suspicious activity near this supply room.
Of the following, which is the MOST reasonable way to carry out your supervisor's direction?

    A. Check the supply room regularly at half-hour intervals
    B. Make frequent checks of the supply room at irregular intervals
    C. Station yourself by the door of the supply room and stay at this post all night
    D. Find a hidden spot from which you can watch the supply room and stay there all night

22. You are on duty at a vehicle entrance to a hospital. Parking space on the hospital grounds is strictly limited, and no one is ever allowed to park there unless they have an official parking permit. You have just stopped a driver who does not have a parking permit, but he explains that
he is a doctor and he has a patient in the hospital. What should you do?

A. Let him park since he has explained that he is a doctor
B. Ask in a friendly way, *"Can I check your identification?"*
C. Call the Information Desk to make sure there is such a patient in the hospital
D. Tell the driver politely but firmly that he will have to park somewhere else

23. You are on duty at a public building. A man was just mugged on a stairway. The mugger took the man's wallet and started to run down the stairs but tripped and fell. Now the mugger is lying unconscious at the bottom of the stairs and bleeding from the mouth.
The FIRST thing you should do is to

A. search him to see if he is carrying any other stolen property
B. pick him up and carry him away from the stairs
C. try and revive him for questioning
D. put in a call for an ambulance and police assistance

24. After someone breaks into an employee's locker at a public building, you interview the employee to determine what is missing from the locker. The employee becomes hysterical and asks why you are *wasting time with all these questions* instead of going after the thief.
The MOST reasonable thing for you to do is

A. tell the employee that it is very important to have an accurate description of the missing articles
B. quietly tell the employee to calm down and stop interfering with your work
C. explain to the employee that you are only doing what you were told to do and that you don't make the rules
D. assure the employee that there are a lot of people working on the case and that someone else is probably arresting the thief right now

25. You are on duty at a public building. An employee reports that a man has just held her up and taken her money. The employee says that the man was about 25 years old, with short blond hair and a pale complexion and was wearing blue jeans.
Of the following additional facts, which one would probably be MOST valuable to officers searching the building for the suspect?

A. The man was wearing dark glasses.
B. He had on a green jacket.
C. He was about 5 feet 8 inches tall.
D. His hands and fingernails were very dirty.

26. When the fire alarm goes off, it is your job as a special officer (security officer) to see that all employees leave the building quickly by the correct exits. A fire alarm has just sounded, and you are checking the offices on one of the floors. A supervisor in one office tells you, *"This is probably just another fire drill. I've sent my office staff out, but I don't want to stop my own work."*
What should you do?

A. Insist politely but firmly that the supervisor must obey the fire rules.
B. Tell the supervisor that it is all right this time but that the rules must be followed in the future.
C. Tell the supervisor that he is under arrest.
D. Allow the supervisor to do as he sees fit since he is in charge of his own office.

27. You are on duty on the main floor of a public building. You have been informed that a briefcase has just been stolen from an office on the tenth floor. You see a man getting off the elevator with a briefcase that matches the description of the one that was stolen. What is the FIRST action you should take?

    A. Arrest the man and take him to the nearest public station
    B. Stop the man and say politely that you want to take a look at the briefcase
    C. Take the briefcase from the man and tell him that he cannot have it back unless he can prove that it is his
    D. Do not stop the man but note down his description and the exact time he got off the elevator

28. You are on duty at a welfare center. You have been told that two clients are arguing with a caseworker and making loud threats. You go to the scene, but the caseworker tells you that everything is now under control. The two clients, who are both mean-looking characters, are still there but seem to be acting normally.
    What SHOULD you do?

    A. Apologize for having made a mistake and go away.
    B. Arrest the two men for having caused a disturbance.
    C. Insist on standing by until the interview is over, then escort the two men from the building.
    D. Leave the immediate scene but watch for any further developments.

29. You are on duty at a welfare center. A client comes up to you and says that two men just threatened him with a knife and made him give them his money. The client has alcohol on his breath and he is shabbily dressed. He points out the two men he says took the money.
    Of the following, which is the BEST action to take?

    A. Arrest the two men on the client's complaint.
    B. Ignore the client's complaint since he doesn't look as if he could have had any money.
    C. Suggest to the client that he may be imagining things.
    D. Investigate and find out what happened.

Questions 30-35.

DIRECTIONS: Answer Questions 30 through 35 on the basis of the information given in the passage below. Assume that all questions refer to the same state described in the passage.

    The courts and the police consider an "offense" as any conduct that is punishable by a fine or imprisonment. Such offenses include many kinds of acts - from behavior that is merely annoying, like throwing a noisy party that keeps everyone awake, all the way up to violent acts like murder. The law classifies offenses according to the penalties that are provided for them. In one state, minor offenses are called "violations." A violation is punishable by a fine of not more than $250 or imprisonment of not more than. 15 days, or both. The annoying behavior mentioned above is an example of a violation. More serious offenses are classified as "crimes." Crimes are classified by the kind of penalty that is provided. A "misdemeanor" is a crime that is punishable by a fine of not more than $1,000 or by imprisonment of not more than one year, or both. Examples of misdemeanors include stealing something with a value of $100 or less, turning in a false alarm, or illegally possessing less than 1/8 of an ounce of a dangerous drug. A "felony" is a criminal offense punishable by imprisonment of more than one year. Murder is clearly a felony.

30. According to the above passage, any act that is punishable by imprisonment or by a fine is called a(n)

    A. offense   B. violation   C. crime   D. felony

31. According to the above passage, which of the following is classified as a crime?

    A. Offense punishable by 15 days imprisonment
    B. Minor offense
    C. Violation
    D. Misdemeanor

32. According to the above passage, if a person guilty of burglary can receive a prison sentence of 7 years or more, burglary would be classified as a

    A. violation   B. misdemeanor
    C. felony   D. violent act

33. According to the above passage, two offenses that would BOTH be classified as misdemeanors are

    A. making unreasonable noise and stealing a $90 bicycle
    B. stealing a $75 radio and possessing 1/16 of an ounce of heroin
    C. holding up a bank and possessing 1/4 of a pound of marijuana
    D. falsely reporting a fire and illegally double-parking

34. The above passage says that offenses are classified according to the penalties provided for them.
    On the basis of clues in the passage, who probably decides what the maximum penalties should be for the different kinds of offenses?

    A. The State lawmakers   B. The City police
    C. The Mayor   D. Officials in Washington, B.C.

35. Of the following, which BEST describes the subject matter of the passage?

    A. How society deals with criminals
    B. How offenses are classified
    C. Three types of criminal behavior
    D. The police approach to offenders

KEY (CORRECT ANSWERS)

1.	C	16.	B
2.	C	17.	B
3.	B	18.	C
4.	D	19.	D
5.	B	20.	C
6.	A	21.	B
7.	B	22.	D
8.	D	23.	D
9.	C	24.	A
10.	C	25.	C
11.	A	26.	A
12.	D	27.	B
13.	A	28.	D
14.	C	29.	D
15.	B	30.	A

31. D
32. C
33. B
34. A
35. B

TEST 2

DIRECTIONS: Each question or incomplete statement is followed by several suggested answers or completions. Select the one that BEST answers the question or completes the statement. *PRINT THE LETTER OF THE CORRECT ANSWER IN THE SPACE AT THE RIGHT.*

Questions 1-5.

DIRECTIONS: Questions 1 through 5 are based on the drawing below showing a view of a waiting area in a public building.

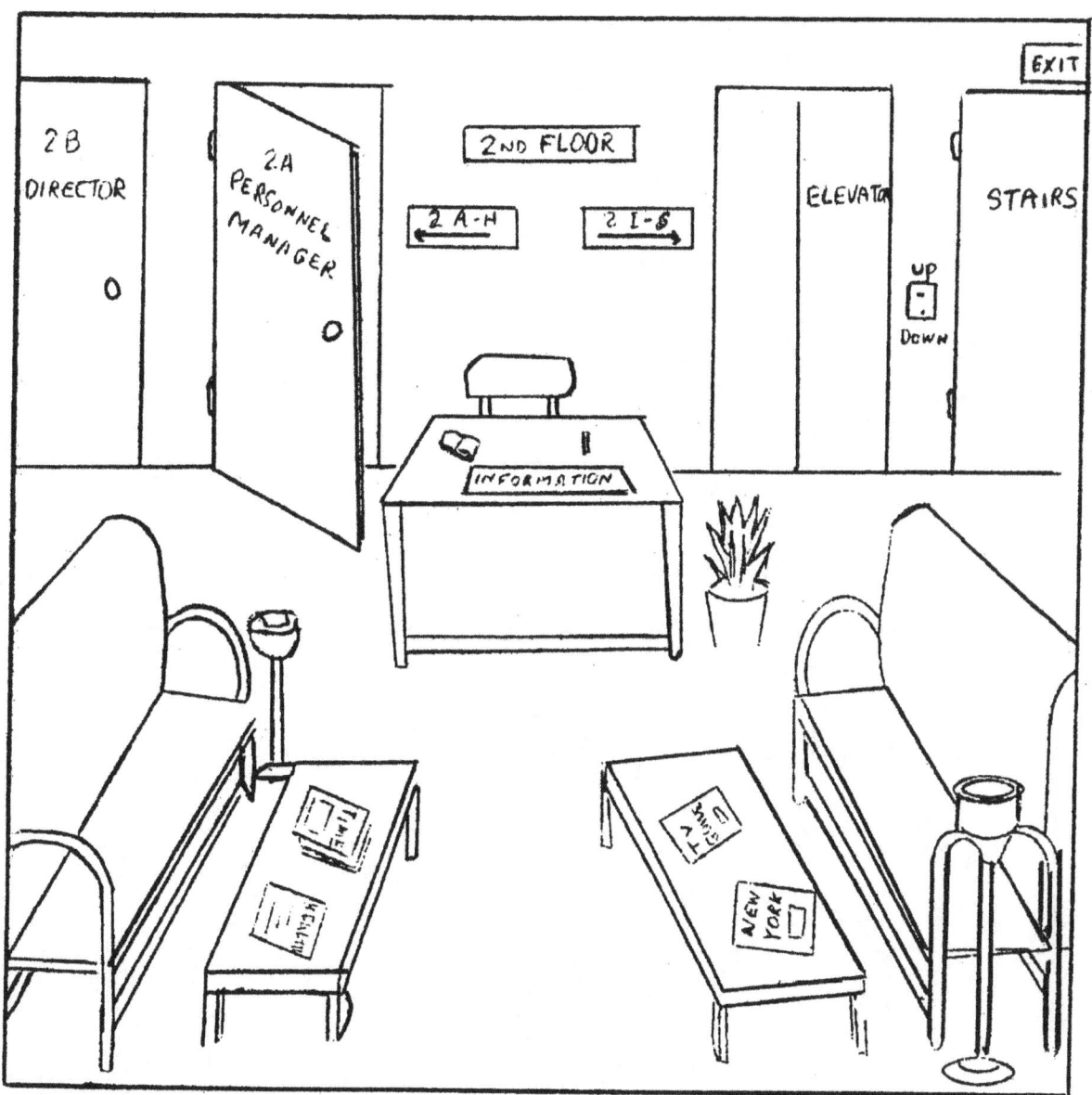

1. A desk is shown in the drawing. Which of the following is on the desk? A(n)

    A. plant
    B. telephone
    C. In-Out file
    D. *Information* sign

1.____

2. On which floor is the waiting area?

   A. Basement
   B. Main floor
   C. Second floor
   D. Third floor

3. The door IMMEDIATELY TO THE RIGHT of the desk is a(n)

   A. door to the Personnel Office
   B. elevator door
   C. door to another corridor
   D. door to the stairs

4. Among the magazines on the tables in the waiting area are

   A. TIME and NEWSWEEK
   B. READER'S DIGEST and T.V. GUIDE
   C. NEW YORK and READER'S DIGEST
   D. TIME and T.V. GUIDE

5. One door is partly open. This is the door to

   A. the Director's office
   B. the Personnel Manager's office
   C. the stairs
   D. an unmarked office

Questions 6-9.

DIRECTIONS: Questions 6 through 9 are based on the drawing below showing the contents of a male suspect's pockets.

CONTENTS OF A MALE SUSPECT'S POCKETS

6. The suspect had a slip in his pockets showing an appointment at an out-patient clinic on   6._____

   A. February 9, 2013 B. September 2, 2013
   C. February 19, 2013 D. September 12, 2013

7. The MP3 player that was found on the suspect was made by   7._____

   A. RCA   B. GE   C. Sony   D. Zenith

8. The coins found in the suspect's pockets have a TOTAL value of   8._____

   A. 56¢   B. 77¢   C. $1.05   D. $1.26

9. All except one of the following were found in the suspect's pockets.   9._____
   Which was NOT found? A

   A. ticket stub   B. comb
   C. subway fare   D. pen

Questions 10-18

DIRECTIONS: In answering Questions 10 through 18, assume that *you* means a special officer (security officer) on duty. Your basic responsibilities are safeguarding people and property and maintaining order in the area to which you are assigned. You are in uniform, and you are not armed. You keep in touch with your supervisory station either by telephone or by a two-way radio (a walkie-talkie).

10. You are on duty at a center run by the Department of Social Services. Two teenaged   10._____
    boys are on their way out of the center. As they go past you, they look at you and laugh, and one makes a remark to you in Spanish. You do not understand Spanish, but you suspect it was a nasty remark.
    What SHOULD you do?

    A. Give the boys a lecture about showing respect for a uniform.
    B. Tell the boys that they had better stay away from the center from now on.
    C. Call for an interpreter and insist that the boy repeat the remark to the interpreter.
    D. Let the boys go on their way since they have done nothing requiring your intervention.

11. You are on duty at a shelter run by the Department of Social Services. You know that   11._____
    many of the shelter clients have drinking problems, drug problems, or mental health problems. You get a call for assistance from a caseworker who says a fight has broken out. When you arrive on the scene, you see that about a dozen clients are engaged in a free-for-all and that two or three of them have pulled knives.
    The BEST course of action is to

    A. call for additional assistance and order all bystanders away from the area
    B. jump into the center of the fighting group and try to separate the fighters
    C. pick up a heavy object and start swinging at anybody who has a knife
    D. try to find out what clients started the fight and place them under arrest

12. You have been assigned to duty at a children's shelter run by the Department of Social Services. The children range in age from 6 to 15, and many of them are at the shelter because they have no homes to go to.
    Of the following, which is the BEST attitude for you to take in dealing with these youngsters?

    A. Assume that they admire and respect anyone in uniform and that they will not usually give you much trouble
    B. Assume that they fear and distrust anyone in uniform and that they are going to give you a hard time unless you act tough
    C. Expect that many of them are going to become juvenile delinquents because of their bad backgrounds and that you should be suspicious of everything they do
    D. Expect that many of them may be emotionally upset and that you should be alert for unusual behavior

13. You are on duty outside the emergency room of a hospital. You notice that an old man has been sitting on a bench outside the room for a long time. He arrived alone, and he has not spoken to anyone at all.
    What SHOULD you do?

    A. Pay no attention to him since he is not bothering anyone.
    B. Tell him to leave since he does not seem to have any business there.
    C. Ask him if you can help him in any way.
    D. Do not speak to him, but keep an eye on him.

14. You are patrolling a section of a public building. An elderly woman carrying a heavy shopping bag asks you if you would watch the shopping bag for her while she keeps an appointment in the building.
    What SHOULD you do?

    A. Watch the shopping bag for her since her appointment probably will not take long.
    B. Refuse her request, explaining that your duties keep you on the move.
    C. Agree to her request just to be polite, but then continue your patrol after the woman is out of sight.
    D. Find a bystander who will agree to watch the shopping bag for her.

15. You are on duty at a public building. It is nearly 6:00 P.M., and most employees have left for the day.
    You see two well-dressed men carrying an office calculating machine out of the building. You SHOULD

    A. stop them and ask for an explanation
    B. follow them to see where they are going
    C. order them to put down the machine and leave the building immediately
    D. take no action since they do not look like burglars

16. You are on duty patrolling a public building. You have just tripped on the stairs and turned your ankle. The ankle hurts and is starting to swell.
    What is the BEST thing to do?

A. Take a taxi to a hospital emergency room, and from there have a hospital employee call your supervisor to explain the situation.
B. First try soaking your foot in cold water for half an hour, then go off duty if you really cannot walk at all.
C. Report the situation to your supervisor, explaining that you need prompt medical attention for your ankle.
D. Find a place where you can sit until you are due to go off duty, then have a doctor look at your ankle.

17. One of your duties as a special officer (security officer) on night patrol in a public building is to check the washrooms to see that the taps are turned off and that there are no plumbing leaks.
Of the following possible reasons for this inspection, which is probably the MOST important reason?

    A. If the floor gets wet, someone might slip and fall the next morning.
    B. A running water tap might be a sign that there is an intruder in the building.
    C. A washroom flood could leak through the ceilings and walls below and cause a lot of damage.
    D. Leaks must be reported quickly so that repairs can be scheduled as soon as possible.

17.____

18. You are on duty at a public building. A department supervisor tells you that someone has left a suspicious-looking package in the hallway on his floor. You investigate, and you hear ticking in the parcel. You think it could be a bomb.
The FIRST thing you should do is to

    A. rapidly question employees on this floor to get a description of the person who left the package
    B. write down the description of the package and the name of the department supervisor
    C. notify your security headquarters that there may be a bomb in the building and that all personnel should be evacuated
    D. pick up the package carefully and remove it from the building as quickly as you can

18.____

Questions 19-22.

DIRECTIONS: Answer Questions 19 through 22 on the basis of the Fact Situation and the Report of Arrest form below. Questions 19 through 22 ask how the report form should be filled in based on the information given in the Fact Situation.

FACT SITUATION

Jesse Stein is a special officer (security officer) who is assigned to a welfare center at 435 East Smythe Street, Brooklyn. He was on duty there Thursday morning, February 1. At 10:30 A.M., a client named Jo Ann Jones, 40 years old, arrived with her ten-year-old son, Peter. Another client, Mary Alice Wiell, 45 years old, immediately began to insult Mrs. Jones. When Mrs. Jones told her to "go away," Mrs. Wiell pulled out a long knife. The special officer (security officer) intervened and requested Mrs. Wiell to drop the knife. She would not, and he had to use necessary force to disarm her. He arrested her on charges of disorderly conduct, harassment, and possession of a dangerous weapon. Mrs. Wiell lives at 118 Heally Street,

Brooklyn, Apartment 4F, and she is unemployed. The reason for her aggressive behavior is not known.

```
REPORT OF ARREST
01) _____     (08) _____
    (Prisoner's surname) (first) (initial)      (Precinct)
02) _____     (09) _____
    (Address)                                  (Date of arrest)
                                               (Month, Day)
03) _____ (04) _____ (05) ____  (10) _____
    (Date of birth)   (Age)      (Sex)         (Time of arrest)
06) _____ (07) _____    (11) _____
    (Occupation)     (Where employed)          (Place of arrest)

(12) _____
     (Specific offenses)

(13) _____ (14) _____
     (Arresting Officer)                   (Officer's No.)
```

19. What entry should be made in Blank 01?

    A. Jo Ann Jones   B. Jones, Jo Ann
    C. Mary Wiell   D. Wiell, Mary A.

20. Which of the following should be entered in Blank 04?

    A. 40   B. 40's   C. 45   D. Middle-aged

21. Which of the following should be entered in Blank 09?

    A. Wednesday, February 1, 10:30 A.M.
    B. February 1
    C. Thursday morning, February 2
    D. Morning, February 4

22. Of the following, which would be the BEST entry to make in Blank 11?

    A. Really Street Welfare Center
    B. Brooklyn
    C. 435 E. Smythe St., Brooklyn
    D. 118 Heally St., Apt. 4F

Questions 23-27.

DIRECTIONS: Answer Questions 23 through 27 on the basis of the information given in the Report of Loss or Theft that appears below.

```
REPORT OF LOSS OR THEFT          Date: 12/4      Time: 9:15 a.m.
Complaint made by: Richard Aldridge        ☐ Owner
                   306 S. Walter St.       ☒ Other - explain:
                                           Head of Accty. Dept.

Type of property: Computer                 Value: $550.00
Description: Dell
Location: 768 N Margin Ave., Accounting Dept., 3rd Floor
Time: Overnight 12/3 - 12/4
Circumstances: Mr. Aldridge reports he arrived at work 8:45 A.M.,
found office door open and machine missing. Nothing else reported
missing. I investigated and found signs of forced entry: door lock
was broken.        Signature of Reporting Officer: B.L. Ramirez
Notify:
  ☐ Building & Grounds Office, 768 N. Margin Ave.
  ☐ Lost Property Office, 110 Brand Ave.
  ☒ Security Office, 703 N. Wide Street
```

23. The person who made this complaint is

    A. a secretary   B. a security officer
    C. Richard Aldridge   D. B.L. Ramirez

24. The report concerns a computer that has been

    A. lost   B. damaged   C. stolen   D. sold

25. The person who took the computer probably entered the office through

    A. a door   B. a window   C. the roof   D. the basement

26. When did the head of the Accounting Department first notice that the computer was missing?

    A. December 4 at 9:15 A.M.   B. December 4 at 8:45 A.M.
    C. The night of December 3   D. The night of December 4

27. The event described in the report took place at

    A. 306 South Walter Street   B. 768 North Margin Avenue
    C. 110 Brand Avenue   D. 703 North Wide Street

8 (#2)

Questions 28-33.

DIRECTIONS: Answer Questions 28 through 33 on the basis of the instructions, the code, and the sample question given below.

Assume that a special officer (security officer) at a certain location is equipped with a two-way radio to keep him in constant touch with his security headquarters. Radio messages and replies are given in code form, as follows:

Radio Code for Situation	J	P	M	F	B
Radio Code for Action to be Taken	o	r	a	z	q
Radio Response for Action Being Taken	1	2	3	4	5

Assume that each of the above capital letters is the radio code for a particular type of situation, that the small letter below each capital letter is the radio code for the action a special officer (security officer) is directed to take, and that the number directly below each small letter is the radio response a special officer (security officer) should make to indicate what action was actually taken.

In each of the following Questions 28 through 33, the code letter for the action directed (Column 2) and the code number for the action taken (Column 3) should correspond to the capital letters in Column 1.

If only Column 2 is different from Column 1, mark your answer A.

If only Column 3 is different from Column 1, mark your answer B.

If both Column 2 and Column 3 are different from Column 1, mark your answer C.

If both Columns 2 and 3 are the same as Column 1, mark your answer D.

SAMPLE QUESTION

Column 1	Column 2	Column 3
JPFMB	orzaq	12453

The code letters in Column 2 are correct, but the numbers 53 in Column 3 should be 35. Therefore, the answer is B.

	Column 1	Column 2	Column 3	
28.	PBFJM	rqzoa	25413	28._____
29.	MPFBJ	zrqao	32541	29._____
30.	JBFPM	oqzra	15432	30._____
31.	BJPMF	qaroz	51234	31._____
32.	PJFMB	rozaq	21435	32._____
33.	FJBMP	zoqra	41532	33._____

Questions 34-40.

DIRECTIONS: Questions 34 through 40 are based on the instructions given below. Study the instructions and the sample question; then answer Questions 34 through 40 on the basis of this information

INSTRUCTIONS:

In each of the following Questions 34 through 40, the 3-line name and address in Column 1 is the master-list entry, and the 3-line entry in Column 2 is the information to be checked against the master list.

If there is one line that does not match, mark your answer A.

If there are two lines that do not match, mark your answer B.

If all three lines do not match, mark your answer C.

If the lines all match exactly, mark your answer D.

SAMPLE QUESTION:

Column 1
Mark L. Field
11-09 Prince Park Blvd.
Bronx, N.Y. 11402

Column 2
Mark L. Field
11-99 Prince Park
Bronx, N.Y. 11401

The first lines in each column match exactly. The second lines do not match, since 11-09 does not match 11-99 and Blvd. does not match Way. The third lines do not match either, since 11402 does not match 11401. Therefore, there are two lines that do not match and the correct answer is B.

	Column 1	Column 2	
34.	Jerome A. Jackson 1243 14th Avenue New York, N.Y. 10023	Jerome A. Johnson 1234 14th Avenue New York, N.Y. 10023	34._____
35.	Sophie Strachtheim 33-28 Connecticut Ave. Far Rockaway, N.Y. 11697	Sophie Strachtheim 33-28 Connecticut Ave. Far Rockaway, N.Y. 11697	35._____
36.	Elisabeth N.T. Gorrell 256 Exchange St. New York, N.Y. 10013	Elizabeth N.T. Gorrell 256 Exchange St. New York, N.Y. 10013	36._____
37.	Maria J. Gonzalez 7516 E. Sheepshead Rd. Brooklyn, N.Y. 11240	Maria J. Gonzalez 7516 N. Shepshead Rd. Brooklyn, N.Y. 11240	37._____
38.	Leslie B. Brautenweiler 21 57A Seller Terr. Flushing, N.Y. 11367	Leslie B. Brautenwieler 21-75A Seiler Terr. Flushing, N.J. 11367	38._____

39. Rigoberto J. Peredes   Rigoberto J. Peredes   39. ____
    157 Twin Towers, #18F   157 Twin Towers, #18F
    Tottenville, S.I., N.Y.   Tottenville, S.I., N.Y.

40. Pietro F. Albino   Pietro F. Albina   40. ____
    P.O. Box 7548   P.O. Box 7458
    Floral Park, N.Y. 11005   Floral Park, N.Y. 11005

KEY (CORRECT ANSWERS)

1.	D	11.	A	21.	B	31.	A
2.	C	12.	D	22.	C	32.	D
3.	B	13.	C	23.	C	33.	A
4.	D	14.	B	24.	C	34.	B
5.	B	15.	A	25.	A	35.	D
6.	A	16.	C	26.	B	36.	A
7.	C	17.	C	27.	B	37.	A
8.	D	18.	C	28.	D	38.	C
9.	D	19.	D	29.	C	39.	D
10.	D	20.	C	30.	B	40.	B

EXAMINATION SECTION
TEST 1

DIRECTIONS: Each question or incomplete statement is followed by several suggested answers or completions. Select the one that BEST answers the question or completes the statement. *PRINT THE LETTER OF THE CORRECT ANSWER IN THE SPACE AT THE RIGHT.*

1. Upon arriving at the scene of an accident in which a pedestrian was struck and killed by an automobile, an officer's first action was to clear the scene of spectators.
   Of the following, the PRINCIPAL reason for this action is that
   A. important evidence may be inadvertently destroyed by the crowd
   B. this is a fundamental procedure in first aid work
   C. the operator of the vehicle may escape in the crowd
   D. witnesses will speak more freely if other persons are not present

    1.____

2. In questioning witnesses, an officer is instructed to avoid leading questions or questions that will suggest the answer.
   Accordingly, when questioning a witness about the appearance of a suspect, it would be BEST for him to ask:
   A. What kind of hat did he wear?   B. Did he wear a felt hat?
   C. What did he wear?   D. Didn't he wear a hat?

    2.____

3. The only personal description the police have of a particular criminal was made several years ago.
   Of the following, the item in the description that will be MOST useful in identifying him at the present time is the
   A. color of his eyes   B. color of his hair
   C. number of teeth   D. weight

    3.____

4. Crime statistics indicate that property crimes such as larceny, burglary, and robbery are more numerous during winter months than in summer.
   The one of the following explanations that MOST adequately accounts for this situation is that
   A. human needs, such as clothing, food, heat, and shelter, are greater in winter
   B. criminal tendencies are aggravated by climatic changes
   C. there are more hours of darkness in winter and such crimes are usually committed under cover of darkness
   D. urban areas are more densely populated during winter months, affording greater opportunity for such crimes

    4.____

5. When automobile tire tracks are to be used as evidence, a plaster cast is made of them.
   Of the following, the MOST probable reason for taking a photograph is that
   A. photographs can be duplicated more easily than castings
   B. less skill is required for photographing than casting
   C. the tracks may be damaged in the casting process
   D. photographs are more easily transported than castings

6. It is generally recommended that an officer, in lifting a revolver that is to be sent to the police laboratory for ballistics tests and fingerprint examination, do so by insetting a pencil through the trigger guard rather than into the barrel of the weapon.
   The reason for preferring this procedure is that
   A. every precaution must be taken not to eliminate fingerprints on the weapon
   B. there is a danger of accidentally discharging the weapon by placing the pencil in the barrel
   C. the pencil may make scratches inside the barrel that will interfere with the ballistics tests
   D. a weapon can more easily be lifted by the trigger guard

7. PHYSICIAN is to PATIENT as ATTORNEY is to
   A. court   B. client   C. counsel   D. judge

8. JUDGE is to SENTENCE as JURY is to
   A. court   B. foreman   C. defendant   D. verdict

9. REVERSAL is to AFFIRMANCE as CONVICTION is to
   A. appeal   B. acquittal   C. error   D. mistrial

10. GENUINE is to TRUE as SPURIOUS is to
    A. correct   B. conceived   C. false   D. speculative

11. ALLEGIANCE is to LOYALTY as TREASON is to
    A. felony   B. faithful   C. obedience   D. rebellion

12. CONCUR is to AGREE as DIFFER is to
    A. coincide   B. dispute   C. join   D. repeal

13. A person who has an uncontrollable desire to steal without need is called a
    A. dipsomaniac   B. kleptomaniac
    C. monomaniac   D. pyromaniac

14. In the sentence, "The placing of any inflammable substance in any building or the placing of any device or contrivence capable of producing fire, for the purpose of causing a fire is an attempt to burn," the MISSPELLED word is
    A. inflammable   B. substance   C. device   D. contrivence

15. In the sentence, "The word 'break' also means obtaining an entrance into a building by any artifice used for that purpose, or by colussion with any person therein," the MISSPELLED word is
    A. obtaining   B. entrance   C. artifice   D. colussion

    15.____

16. In the sentence, "Any person who with intent to provoke a breech of the peace causes a disturbance or is offensive to others may be deemed to have committed disorderly conduct," the MISSPELLED word is
    A. breech   B. disturbance   C. offensive   D. committed

    16.____

17. In the sentence, "When the offender inflicts a grevious harm upon the person from whose possession, or in his presence, property is taken, he is guilty of robbery, the MISSPELLED word is
    A. offender   B. grevious   C. possession   D. presence

    17.____

18. In the sentence, "A person who wilfully encourages or advises another person in attempting to take the latter's life is guilty of a felony," the MISSPELLED word is
    A. wilfully   B. encourages   C. advises   D. attempting

    18.____

19. The treatment to be given the offender cannot alter the fact of his offense; but we can take measures to reduce the chances of similar acts in the future. We should banish the criminal, not in order to exact revenge nor directly to encourage reform, but to deter him and others from further illegal attacks on society.
    According to this paragraph, the PRINCIPAL reason for punishing criminals is to
    A. prevent the commission of future crimes
    B. remove them safely from society
    C. avenge society
    D. teach them that crime does not pay

    19.____

20. Even the most comprehensive and best substantiated summaries of the total volume of criminal acts would not contribute greatly to an understanding of the varied social and biological factors which are sometimes assumed to enter into crime causation, nor would they indicate with any degree of precision the needs of police forces in combating crime.
    According to this statement,
    A. crime statistics alone do not determine the needs of police forces in combating crime
    B. crime statistics are essential to a proper understanding of the social factors of crime
    C. social and biological factor which enter the crime causation have little bearing on police needs
    D. a knowledge of the social and biological factors of crime is essential to a proper understanding of crime statistics

    20.____

21. The police officer's art consists in applying and enforcing a multitude of laws and ordinances in such degree or proportion and in such manner that the greatest degree of social protection will be secured. The degree of enforcement and the method of application will vary with each neighborhood and community.
According to the foregoing paragraph,
   A. each neighborhood or community must judge for itself to what extent the law is to be enforced
   B. a police officer should only enforce those laws which are designed to give the greatest degree of social protection
   C. the manner and intensity of law enforcement is not necessarily the same in all communities
   D. all laws and ordinances must be enforced in a community with the same degree of intensity

22. Police control in the sense of regulating the details of police operations involves such matters as the technical means for so organizing the available personnel that competent police leadership, when secured, can operate effectively. It is concerned not so much with the extent to which popular controls can be trusted to guide and direct the course of police protection a with the administrative relationships which should exist between the component parts of the police organism.
According to the foregoing statement, police control is
   A. solely a matter of proper personnel assignment
   B. the means employed to guide and direct the course of police protection
   C. principally concerned with the administrative relationships between units of a police organization
   D. the sum total of means employed in rendering police protection

23. Two patrol cars hurry to the scene of an accident from different directions. The first proceeds at the rate of 45 miles per hour and arrives in four minutes. Although the second car travels over a route which is three-fourths of a mile longer, it arrives at the scene only a half-minute later.
The speed of the second car, expressed in miles per hour, is
   A. 50   B. 55   C. 60   D. 65

24. A motorcycle officer issued 72 traffic summonses in January, 60 in February and 83 in March.
In order to average 75 summonses per month for the four months of January, February, March, and April, during April he will have to issue _____ summonses.
   A. 80   B. 85   C. 90   D. 95

25. In a unit of the Police Department to which 40 officers are assigned, the sick report record during 2022 was as follows: 1 was absent 8 days, 5 were absent 3 days each, 4 were absent 5 days each, 10 were absent 2 days each, 8 were absent 4 days each, 5 were absent 1 day each.
The average number of days on sick report for all the members of this unit is MOST NEARLY
   A. ½   B. 1   C. 2 ½   D. 3

Questions 26-30.

DIRECTIONS: Column I lists various statements of fact. Column II is a list of crimes. Next to the numbers corresponding to the number preceding the statements of fact in Column I, place the letter preceding the crime listed in Column II with which Jones should be charged. In answering these questions, the following definitions of crimes should be applied, bearing in mind that ALL elements contained in the definitions must be present in order to charge a person with that crime.

BURGLARY is breaking and entering a building with intent to commit some crime therein. EMBEZZLEMENT is the appropriation to one's use of another's property which has been entrusted to one's care or which has come lawfully into one's possession. EXTORTION is taking or obtaining property from another with his consent, induced by a wrongful use of force or fear. LARCENY is taking and carrying away the personal property of another with intent to deprive or defraud the true owner of the use and benefit of such property. ROBBERY is the unlawful taking of the personal property of another from his person or in his presence by force or violence, or fear of injury.

COLUMN I

26. Jones, believing Smith had induced his wife to leave him, went to Smith's home armed with a knife with which he intended to assault Smith. When his knock was unanswered, he forced open the door of Smith's home and entered but, finding the house empty, he threw away the knife and left.

27. Jones was employed as a collection agent by Smith. When Smith refused to reimburse him for certain expenses he claimed to have incurred in connection with his work, Jones deducted this amount from sums he had collected for Smith.

28. Jones spent the night in a hotel. During the night he left his room, went downstairs to the desk, stole money and returned to his room.

29. Jones, a building inspector, found that the elevators in Smith's building were being operated without a permit. He threatened to report the matter and have the elevators shut down unless Smith paid him a sum of money. Smith paid the amount demanded

30. Jones held-up Smith on the street and, pointing a revolve at him, demanded his money. Smith, without resisting, handed Jones his money. When Jones was apprehended, it was discovered that the revolver was a toy.

COLUMN II

A. burglary
B. embezzlement
C. extortion
D. larceny
E. robbery
F. no crime

26.____
27.____
28.____
29.____
30.____

Questions 31-40.

DIRECTIONS: Questions 31 through 40 consist of statements from which a term is missing. Each of these statements can be completed correctly with one of the terms in the following list. In the space opposite the number corresponding to the number of the question, place the LETTER preceding the term in the following list which MOST accurately completes the statement.

- A. affidavit
- B. appeal
- C. arraignment
- D. arrest
- E. bench warrant
- F. habeas corpus
- G. indictment
- H. injunction
- I. sentence
- J. subpoena

31. A _____ is a writ calling witnesses to court. 31._____

32. _____ is a method used to obtain a review of a case in court of superior jurisdiction. 32._____

33. A judgment passed by a court on a person on trial as a criminal offender is called a _____. 33._____

34. _____ is a writ or order requiring a person to refrain from a particular act. 34._____

35. _____ is the name given to a writ commanding the bringing of the body of a certain person before a certain court. 35._____

36. A _____ is a court order directing that an offender be brought into court. 36._____

37. The calling of a defendant before the court to answer an accusation is called _____. 37._____

38. The accusation in writing, presented by the grand jury to a competent court charging a person with a public offense is an _____. 38._____

39. A sworn declaration in writing is an _____. 39._____

40. _____ is the taking of a person into custody for the purpose of holding him to answer a criminal charge. 40._____

Questions 41-55.

DIRECTIONS: Questions 41 through 55 consist of statements from which a term is missing. Each of these statements can be completed correctly with one of the terms in the following list. In the space opposite the number corresponding to the number of the question, place the LETTER preceding the term in the following list which MOST accurately completes the statement.

A. accessory   B. accomplice   C. alibi
D. autopsy   E. ballistics   F. capital
G. confidence man H. commission   I. conspiracy
J. corroborated K. grand jury   L. homicide
M. misdemeanors N. penology   O. perjury

41. _____ is the dissection of a dead human body to determine the cause of death. 41._____

42. The general term which mean the killing of one person by another is _____. 42._____

43. _____ is the science of the punishment of crime. 43._____

44. False swearing constitutes the crime of _____. 44._____

45. A combination of two or more persons to accomplish a criminal or unlawful act is called _____. 45._____

46. By _____ is meant evidence showing that a defendant was in another place when the crime was committed. 46._____

47. _____ is a term frequently used to describe a person engaged in a kind of swindling operation. 47._____

48. A _____ offense is one for which a life sentence or death penalty is prescribed by law. 48._____

49. A violation of a law may be either an act of omission or an act of _____. 49._____

50. An _____ is a person who is liable to prosecution for the identical offense charged against a defendant on trial. 50._____

51. A person would be an _____ who after the commission of a crime aided in the escape of one he knew to be an offender. 51._____

52. An official body called to hear complaints and to determine whether there is ground for criminal prosecution is known as the _____. 52._____

53. Crimes are generally divided into two classes, namely felonies and _____. 53._____

54. _____ is the science of the motion of projectiles. 54._____

55. Testimony of a witness which is confirmed by another witness is _____. 55._____

Questions 56-60.

DIRECTIONS: Next to the question number which corresponds with the number of each item in Column I, place the letter preceding the adjective in Column II which BEST describes the persons in Column I.

COLUMN I	COLUMN II	
56. A talkative woman	A. abstemious	56.____
	B. pompous	
57. A person on a reducing diet	C. erudite	57.____
	D. benevolent	
58. A scholarly professor	E. docile	58.____
	F. loquacious	
59. A man who seldom speaks	G. indefatigable	59.____
	H. taciturn	
60. A charitable person		60.____

Questions 61-65.

DIRECTIONS: Next to the question number which corresponds with the number preceding each profession in Column I, place the letter preceding the word in Column II which BEST explains the subject of that profession.

COLUMN I	COLUMN II	
61. Geologist	A. animals	61.____
	B. eyes	
62. Oculist	C. feet	62.____
	D. fortune-telling	
63. Podiatrist	E. language	63.____
	F. rocks	
64. Palmist	G. stamps	64.____
	H. woman	
65. Zoologist		65.____

Questions 66-70.

DIRECTIONS: Next to the question number corresponding to the number of each of the words in Column I, place the letter preceding the word in Column II that is MOST NEARLY OPPOSITE to it in meaning.

COLUMN I	COLUMN II	
66. comely	A. beautiful	66.____
	B. cowardly	
67. eminent	C. kind	67.____
	D. sedate	
68. frugal	E. shrewd	68.____
	F. ugly	
69. gullible	G. unknown	69.____
	H. wasteful	
70. valiant		70.____

KEY (CORRECT ANSWERS)

1. A	16. A	31. J	46. C	61. F
2. C	17. B	32. B	47. G	62. B
3. A	18. A	33. I	48. F	63. C
4. C	19. A	34. H	49. H	64. D
5. C	20. A	35. F	50. B	65. A
6. C	21. C	36. E	51. A	66. F
7. B	22. C	37. C	52. L	67. G
8. D	23. A	38. G	53. N	68. H
9. B	24. B	39. A	54. E	69. E
10. C	25. C	40. D	55. K	70. B
11. D	26. A	41. D	56. F	
12. B	27. B	42. M	57. A	
13. B	28. D	43. O	58. C	
14. D	29. C	44. P	59. H	
15. D	30. E	45. J	60. D	

EXAMINATION SECTION
TEST 1

DIRECTIONS: Each question or incomplete statement is followed by several suggested answers or completions. Select the one that BEST answers the question or completes the statement. *PRINT THE LETTER OF THE CORRECT ANSWER IN THE SPACE AT THE RIGHT.*

1. The delivery of an arrested person to his sureties, upon their giving security for his appearance at the time and place designated to submit to the jurisdiction and judgment of the court, is known as
    A. bail
    B. habeas corpus
    C. parole
    D. probation

2. Jones was charged with the murder of Smith. Brown, Jones' landlord, testified at the trial that Jones had in his home a well-equipped laboratory which contained all the necessary chemical for producing the poison which an autopsy showed caused Smith's death.
Brown's testimony constitutes what is called _____ evidence.
    A. corroborative   B. opinion   C. hearsay   D. circumstantial

3. In addressing a class of recruits, a police lieutenant remarked: "Carelessness and failure are twins."
The one of the following that MOST NEARLY expresses his meaning is
    A. negligence seldom accompanies success
    B. incomplete work is careless work
    C. conscientious work is never attended by failure
    D. a conscientious person never makes mistakes

4. In taking a statement from a person who has been shot by an assailant and is not expected to live, police are instructed to ask the person: "Do you believe you are about to die?"
Of the following, the MOST probable reason for this question is
    A. the theory that a person about to die will tell the truth
    B. to determine if the victim is conscious and capable of making a statement
    C. to put the victim mentally at ease and more willing to talk
    D. that the statement could not be used in court if his mind was distraught by the fear of impending death

5. If, while you are on duty at a busy intersection, a pedestrian asks you for directions to a particular place, the BEST course of conduct is to
    A. ignore the question and continue directing operations
    B. tell the pedestrian to ask a patrolman on foot patrol
    C. answer the question in a brief, courteous manner
    D. leave your post only long enough to give clear and adequate directions

2 (#1)

6. In lecturing on the law of arrest, a lieutenant remarked: "To go beyond is as bad as to fall short."
The one of the following which MOST NEARLY expresses his meaning is
   A. never undertake the impossible   B. extremes are not desirable
   C. look before you leap   D. too much success is dangerous

6._____

7. Suppose you are an officer assigned to a patrol precinct. While you are in the vicinity of a school, your attention is called to a man who is selling small packages to school children. You are told that this man distributes similar packages to these same children daily and that he is suspected of dealing in narcotics.
Of the following, the BEST action for you to take is to
   A. pretend to be an addict and attempt to purchase narcotics from him
   B. observe the man's action yourself for several days in order to obtain grounds for arrest
   C. stop and question one or more of the children after they have transacted business with the man
   D. stop and question the man as he leaves the children

7._____

8. In the event of a poison gas attack, civil defense authorities advise civilians to _____ door and windows and go to _____.
   A. open; upper floors   B. close; upper floors
   C. open; the basement   D. close; the basement

8._____

9. The procedure whereby a defendant is brought before a magistrate, informed of the charge against him, and asked how he pleads thereto, is called
   A. arraignment   B. indictment   C. presentment   D. inquisition

9._____

10. A written accusation of a crime presented by a grand jury is called a(n)
    A. commitment   B. arraignment   C. indictment   D. demurrer

10._____

11. The one of the following statements made by a prisoner that is correctly called an alibi is:
    A. "He struck me first."
    B. "I didn't intend to hurt him."
    C. "I was miles away from there at the time."
    D. "I don't remember what happened."

11._____

12. A person who, after the commission of a crime, conceals the defender with the intent that the latter may escape from arrest and trial, is called a(n)
    A. accessory   B. accomplice   C. confederate   D. associate

12._____

13. A sworn statement of fact is called a(n)
    A. affidavit   B. oath
    C. acknowledgment   D. subpoena

13._____

14. The right of trial by jury in the courts of the state is PRIMARILY safeguarded by a provision of
    A. the United States Constitution
    B. the constitution of the state
    C. a state statute
    D. a Federal statute

14.____

15. The task of protecting the President and his family is entrusted PRIMARILY to the
    A. Federal Bureau of Investigation
    B. United States Secret Service
    C. Central Intelligence Agency
    D. District of Columbia Police Department

15.____

16. The coordinating organization for the various Federal agencies engaged in intelligence activities is the
    A. Federal Bureau of Investigation
    B. Federal Security Agency
    C. Mutual Security Agency
    D. Central Intelligence Agency

16.____

17. A drug addict whose arm shows many scars from the injection of a hypodermic needle is MOST apt to be addicted to
    A. heroin   B. cocaine   C. opium   D. marijuana

17.____

18. All of the following drugs are derived from opium EXCEPT
    A. cocaine   B. heroin   C. morphine   D. codeine

18.____

19. In addition to cases of submersion, artificial respiration is a recommended first aid procedure for
    A. sunstroke
    B. chemical poisoning
    C. electric shock
    D. apoplexy

19.____

20. An injury to a muscle or tendon brought about by severe exertion and resulting in pain and stiffness is called a
    A. strain   B. sprain   C. bruise   D. fracture

20.____

21. Of the following kinds of wounds, the one in which there is the LEAST danger of infection is a(n) _____ wound.
    A. abrasive   B. punctured   C. lacerated   D. incised

21.____

22. When a person is found injured on the street, it is generally advisable, pending arrival of a physician, to help prevent fainting or shock by keeping the patient
    A. in a sitting position
    B. lying down with the head level
    C. lying down with the head raised
    D. standing on his feet

22.____

23. When an injured person appears to be suffering from shock, of the following, it is MOST essential to
    A. loosen his clothing
    B. keep him warm
    C. administer a stimulant
    D. place him in a prone position

23.____

24. In the sentence, "Malice was immanent in all his remarks," the word "immanent" means MOST NEARLY
    A. elevated   B. inherent   C. threatening   D. foreign

25. In the sentence, "The extant copies of the document were found in the safe," the word "extant" means MOST NEARLY
    A. existing   B. original   C. forged   D. duplicate

26. In the sentence, "The recruit was more complaisant after the captain spoke to him," the word "complaisant" means MOST NEARLY
    A. calm   B. affable   C. irritable   D. confident

27. In the sentence, "The man was captured under highly creditable circumstances," the word "creditable" means MOST NEARLY
    A. doubtful   B. believable   C. praiseworthy   D. unexpected

28. In the sentence, "His superior officers were more sagacious than he," the word "sagacious" means MOST NEARLY
    A. shrewd   B. obtuse   C. absurd   D. verbose

29. In the sentence, "He spoke with impunity," the word "impunity" means MOST NEARLY
    A. rashness   B. caution   C. without fear   D. immunity

30. In the sentence, "The new patrolman displayed unusual temerity during the emergency," the word "temerity" means MOST NEARLY
    A. fear   B. rashness   C. calmness   D. anxiety

31. In the sentence, "The portions of food were parsimoniously served," the word "parsimoniously" means MOST NEARLY
    A. stingily   B. piously   C. elaborately   D. generously

32. In the sentence, "Generally the speaker's remarks were sententious," the word "sententious" means MOST NEARLY
    A. verbose   B. witty
    C. argumentative   D. pithy

33. In the sentence, "The prisoner was fractious when brought to the station house," the word "fractious" means MOST NEARLY
    A. penitent   B. talkative   C. irascible   D. broken-hearted

34. In the sentence, "The judge was implacable when the attorney pleaded for leniency," the word "implacable" means MOST NEARLY
    A. inexorable   B. disinterested
    C. inattentive   D. indifferent

35. In the sentence, "The court ordered the mendacious statements stricken from the record," the word "mendacious" means MOST NEARLY
    A. begging   B. lying   C. threatening   D. lengthy

36. In the sentence, "The district attorney spoke in a strident voice," the word "strident" means MOST NEARLY
    A. loud
    B. harsh-sounding
    C. sing-song
    D. low

37. In the sentence, "The speaker had a predilection for long sentences," the word "predilection" means MOST NEARLY
    A. aversion
    B. talent
    C. propensity
    D. diffidence

38. In the sentence, "The candidate wants to file his application for preference before it is too late," the word "before" is used as a(n)
    A. preposition
    B. subordinating conjunction
    C. pronoun
    D. adverb

39. The one of the following sentences which is grammatically PREFERABLE to the others is:
    A. Our engineers will go over your blueprints so that you may have no problems in construction.
    B. For a long time he had been arguing that we, not he, are to blame for the confusion.
    C. I worked on this automobile for two hours and still cannot find out what is wrong with it.
    D. Accustomed to all kinds of hardships, fatigue seldom bothers veteran policemen.

40. The plural of
    A. turkey is turkies
    B. cargo is cargoes
    C. bankruptcy is bankruptcys
    D. son-in-law is son-in-laws

41. The abbreviation "viz." means MOST NEARLY
    A. namely
    B. for example
    C. the following
    D. see

42. In the sentence, "A man in a light-grey suit waited thirty-five minutes in the ante-room for the all-important document," the word IMPROPERLY hyphenated is
    A. light-grey
    B. thirty-five
    C. ante-room
    D. all-important

43. The MOST accurate of the following sentences is:
    A. The commissioner, as well as his deputy and various bureau heads, were present.
    B. A new organization of employers and employees have been formed.
    C. One or the other of these men have been selected.
    D. The number of pages in the book is enough to discourage a reader.

44. The MOST accurate of the following sentences is:
    A. Between you and me, I think he is the better man.
    B. He was believed to be me.
    C. Is it us that you wish to see?
    D. The winners are him and her.

45. In the sentence, "The committee favored submiting the amendment to the electorate," the MISSPELLED word is
    A. committee   B. submiting   C. amendment   D. electorate

46. In the sentence, "He maliciously demurred to an ajournment of the proceedings," the MISSPELLED word is
    A. maliciously   B. demurred   C. ajournment   D. proceedings

47. In the sentence, "His innocence at that time is irrelevent in view of his more recent villainous demeanor," the MISSPELLED word is
    A. innocence   B. irrelevent   C. villainous   D. demeanor

48. In the sentence, "The mischievous boys aggrevated the annoyance of their neighbor," the MISSPELLED word is
    A. mischievous   B. aggrevated   C. annoyance   D. neighbor

49. In the sentence, "While his persiverance was commendable, his judgment was debatable, the MISSPELLED word is
    A. persiverance
    B. commendable
    C. judgment
    D. debatable

50. In the sentence, "He was hoping the appeal would facilitate his aquittal," the MISSPELLED word is
    A. hoping   B. appeal   C. facilitate   D. aquittal

51. In the sentence, "It would be preferable for them to persue separate courses," the MISSPELLED word is
    A. preferable   B. persue   C. separate   D. courses

52. In the sentence, "The litigant was complimented on his persistance and achievement," the MISSPELLED word is
    A. litigant
    B. complimented
    C. persistance
    D. achievement

53. In the sentence, "Ocassionally there are discrepancies in the descriptions of miscellaneous items," the MISSPELLED word is
    A. ocassionally
    B. discrepancies
    C. descriptions
    D. miscellaneous

54. In the sentence, "The councilmanic seargent-at-arms enforced the prohibition," the MISSPELLED word is
    A. councilmanic
    B. seargent-at-arms
    C. enforced
    D. prohibition

55. In the sentence, "The teacher had an ingenious device for mantaining attendance," the MISSPELLED word is
    A. ingenious   B. device   C. mantaining   D. attendance

Questions 56-63.

DIRECTIONS: Questions 56 through 63 are to be answered on the basis of the following excerpt from a recorded annual report of the police department. This material should be read first and then referred to in answering these questions, which are to be answered SOLELY on the basis of the material herein contained.

LEGAL BUREAU

One of the more important functions of this bureau is to analyze and furnish the department with pertinent information concerning Federal and State statutes and Local Laws which affect the department, law enforcement or crime prevention. In addition, all measures introduced in the State Legislature and the City Council which may affect this department are carefully reviewed by members of the Legal Bureau and, where necessary, opinions and recommendations thereon are prepared.

Another important function of this office is the prosecution of cases in the Magistrate's Courts. This is accomplished by assignment of attorneys who are members of the Legal Bureau to appear in those cases which are deemed to raise issues of importance to the department or questions of law which require technical presentation to facilitate proper determination; and also in those cases where request is made for such appearances by a magistrate, some other official of the city, or a member of the force. Attorneys are regularly assigned to prosecute all cases in the Women's Court.

Proposed legislation was prepared and sponsored for introduction in the State Legislature and, at this writing, one of these proposals has already been enacted into law and five others are presently on the Governor's desk awaiting executive action. The new law prohibits the sale or possession of a hypodermic syringe or needle by an unauthorized person. The bureau's proposals awaiting executive action pertain to an amendment to the Code of Criminal Procedure prohibiting desk officers from taking bail in gambling cases or in cases mentioned in Section 552, Code of Criminal Procedure; including confidence men and swindlers as jostlers in the Penal Law; prohibiting the sale of switchblade knives of any size to children under 16 and bills extending the licensing period of gunsmiths.

The Legal Bureau has regularly cooperated with the Corporation Counsel and the District Attorneys in respect to matters affecting this department, and has continued to advise and represent the Police Athletic League, the Police Sports Association, the Police Relief Fund, and the Police Pension Fund.

The following is a statistical report of the activities of the bureau during the current year as compared with the previous year:

	Current Year	Previous Year
Memoranda of law prepared	68	83
Legal matters forwarded to corporation counsel	122	144
Letters requesting legal information	756	807
Letters requesting departmental records	139	111
Matters for publication	17	26
Court appearances of members of bureau	4,678	4,621
Conferences	94	103
Lectures at Police Academy	30	33
Reports on proposed legislation	194	255
Deciphering of codes	79	27
Expert testimony	31	16
Notices to court witnesses	55	81
Briefs prepared	22	18
Court papers prepared	258	--

56. One of the functions of the Legal Bureau is to
    A. review and make recommendations on proposed Federal laws affecting law enforcement
    B. prepare opinions on all measures introduced in the State Legislature and the City Council
    C. furnish the Police Department with pertinent information concerning all new Federal and State laws
    D. analyze all laws affecting the work of the Police Department

57. The one of the following that is NOT a function of the Legal Bureau is
    A. law enforcement and crime prevention
    B. prosecution of all cases in Women's Court
    C. advise and represent the Police Sports Association
    D. lecturing at the Police Academy

58. Members of the Legal Bureau frequently appear in Magistrate's Court for the purpose of
    A. defending members of the Police Force
    B. raising issues of importance to the Police Department
    C. prosecuting all offenders arrested by members of the Force
    D. facilitating proper determination of questions of law requiring technical presentation

59. The Legal Bureau sponsored a bill that would
    A. extend the licenses of gunsmiths
    B. prohibit the sale of switchblade knives to children of any size
    C. place confidence men and swindlers in the same category as jostlers in the Penal Law
    D. prohibit desk officers from admitting gamblers, confidence men, and swindlers to bail

9 (#1)

60. From the report, it is NOT reasonable to infer that
    A. fewer bills affecting the Police Department were introduced in the current year
    B. the preparation of court papers was a new activity assumed in the current year
    C. the Code of Criminal Procedure authorizes desk officers to accept bail in certain cases
    D. the penalty for jostling and swindling is the same

60.____

61. According to the statistical report, the activity showing the GREATEST percentage of decrease in the current year as compared to the previous year was
    A. matters for publication
    B. reports on proposed legislation
    C. notices to court witnesses
    D. memoranda of law prepared

61.____

62. According to the statistical report, the activity showing the GREATEST percentage of increase in the current year as compare with the previous year was
    A. court appearances of members of the bureau
    B. giving expert testimony
    C. deciphering of codes
    D. letters requesting departmental records

62.____

63. According to the report, the percentage of bills prepared and sponsored by the Legal Bureau which were passed by the State Legislature and sent to the Governor for approval was APPROXIMATELY
    A. 3.1%
    B. 2.6%
    C. .5%
    D. not capable of determination from the data given

63.____

64. A squad of officers assigned to enforce a new parking regulation in a particular area issued tag summonses on a particular day as follows: four officers issued 16 summonses each; three issued 19 each; one issued 22; seven issued 25 each; eleven issued 28 each; ten issued 30 each; two issued 36 each; one issued 41; and three issued 45 each.
    The average number of summonses issued by a member of this squad was MOST NEARLY
    A. 6.2   B. 17.2   C. 21.0   D. 27.9

64.____

65. A water storage tank is 75 feet long and 30 feet wide and has a depth of 6½ feet. Each cubic foot of the tank holds 9½ gallons.
    The TOTAL capacity of the tank is _____ gallons.
    A. 73,125½   B. 131,625   C. 138,937½   D. 146,250

65.____

66. The price of admission to a PAL entertainment were $2.50 each for adults and $1.00 for children; the turnstile at the entrance showed that 358 persons entered and the gate receipts were $626.50.
The number of children who attended was
   A. 170   B. 175   C. 179   D. 183

66._____

67. A patrol car travels six times as fast as a bicycle.
If the patrol car goes 168 miles in two hours less time than the bicycle requires to go 42 miles, their respective rates of speed are _____ miles per hour.
   A. 36 and 6   B. 42 and 7   C. 63 and 10½   D. 126 and 21

67._____

68. The radiator of an automobile already contains six quarts of a 10% solution of alcohol.
In order to make a mixture of 20% alcohol, it will be necessary to add _____ quarts of alcohol.
   A. ¾   B. 1¾   C. 2½   D. 3

68._____

69. A man received an inheritance of $80,000 and wanted to invest it so that it would produce an annual income sufficient to pay his rent of $400 a month. In order to do this, he will have to receive interest or dividends at the rate of _____% per annum.
   A. 3   B. 4   C. 5¾   D. 6

69._____

70. If the price of a bus ticket varies *directly* as the mileage involved, and a ticket to travel 135 miles costs $29.70, a ticket for a 30-mile trip will cost
   A. $15.20   B. $13.40   C. $6.60   D. $2.20

70._____

71. A man owed a debt of $5,800. After a first payment of $100, he agreed to pay the balance by monthly payments in which each payment after this first would be $20 more than that of the preceding month.
If no interest charge is made, he will have to make, including the first payment, a total of _____ monthly payments.
   A. 16   B. 20   C. 24   D. 28

71._____

72. The written test of a civil service examination has a weight of 30, the oral test a weight of 20, experience a weight of 20, and the physical test a weight of 30. A candidate received ratings of 76 on the written test, 84 on the oral, and 80 for experience.
In order to attain an average of 85 on the examination, his rating on the physical test must be
   A. 86   B. 90   C. 94   D. 98

72._____

73. A family has an income of $3,200 per month. It spends 22% of this amount for rent, 36% for food, 16% for clothing, and 12% for additional household expenses. After meeting these expenses, 50% of the balance is deposited in the bank.
The amount deposited monthly is
   A. $224.00   B. $366.00   C. $448.00   D. $520.00

73._____

11 (#1)

74. Upon retirement last July, an officer bought a farm of 64 acres for $18,000 per acre. He made a down payment of $612,000 and agreed to pay the balance in installments of $7,500 a month commencing on August 1, 2022. Disregarding interest, he will make his LAST payment in
    A. July 2028
    B. August 2030
    C. January 2032
    D. April 2035

75. 40% of those who commit a particular crime are subsequently arrested and convicted. 75% of those committed receive sentences of 10 years or more. Assuming that those arrested for the first time serve less than 10 years, the percentage of those committing this crime who receive sentences of ten years or more is MOST NEARLY
    A. 20%   B. 30%   C. 40%   D. 50%

KEY (CORRECT ANSWERS)

1.	A	21.	D	41.	A	61.	A
2.	D	22.	B	42.	C	62.	C
3.	A	23.	B	43.	D	63.	D
4.	A	24.	B	44.	A	64.	D
5.	C	25.	A	45.	B	65.	C
6.	B	26.	B	46.	C	66.	C
7.	C	27.	C	47.	C	67.	B
8.	B	28.	A	48.	B	68.	A
9.	A	29.	D	49.	A	69.	D
10.	C	30.	B	50.	D	70.	C
11.	C	31.	A	51.	B	71.	B
12.	A	32.	D	52.	C	72.	D
13.	A	33.	C	53.	A	73.	A
14.	B	34.	A	54.	B	74.	A
15.	B	35.	B	55.	C	75.	B
16.	D	36.	B	56.	D		
17.	A	37.	C	57.	A		
18.	A	38.	B	58.	D		
19.	C	39.	A	59.	C		
20.	A	40.	B	60.	D		

EXAMINATION SECTION
TEST 1

DIRECTIONS: Each question or incomplete statement is followed by several suggested answers or completions. Select the one that BEST answers the question or completes the statement. *PRINT THE LETTER OF THE CORRECT ANSWER IN THE SPACE AT THE RIGHT.*

1. During an interview with a witness, the investigator should carefully observe the witness's gestures and facial expressions.
   To interpret the meaning of these actions, the investigator should do all of the following EXCEPT to

   A. try to *read* the situation in which a puzzling gesture is used
   B. ask questions that relate specifically to the gesture
   C. take an educated guess based on past experience
   D. rely on the standard meaning of the gesture

   1._____

2. Of the following, the MOST important skill for a supervisor of investigators to possess is the ability to

   A. communicate effectively
   B. obtain the respect of his staff
   C. remain calm in pressure situations
   D. develop high morale among his subordinates

   2._____

3. Following are three statements concerning the preparation by an investigator of a written statement taken from a witness:
   I. Have each page initialed by the witness
   II. Correct and initial any mistakes in grammar that are made by the witness
   III. Leave space between paragraphs to facilitate the addition of notes and comments.

   Which of the following correctly classifies the above statements into those that are valid and those that are not?

   A. I is valid, but II and III are not.
   B. II and III are valid, but I is not.
   C. III is valid, but I and II are not.
   D. I and II are valid, but III is not.

   3._____

4. Assume, as an investigator, you are questioning an employee of your agency suspected of misstating previous work experience on his employment application. You notice that the employee is reluctant to admit that his previous statements were inaccurate.
   The one of the following that is the BEST method of obtaining the truth from this employee would be for you to

   A. tell him that his job is not in jeopardy
   B. make him feel he is not being criticized
   C. have him discuss the matter with your supervisor
   D. allow him to correct any inaccuracies on his employment application

   4._____

5. If several witnesses describing the same occurrence agree on most details, the investigator should then

   A. determine whether or not these witnesses were in communication with each other
   B. assume that such agreement means that the recollection was correct
   C. assume that the witnesses' observations were incorrect since two or more people usually will not agree on the same details
   D. question the witnesses again, concentrating on the details on which they differ

6. In trying to obtain a statement from a hospitalized individual who is unable to receive visitors, it would be BEST for an investigator

   A. draw up a statement from his own knowledge of the case and ask a hospital staff member to have the patient sign the statement when he is well
   B. contact the patient's family and arrange for an appointment to see the patient as soon as his condition permits
   C. leave a message at the hospital for the patient to contact him when he is available to receive visitors
   D. appear at the hospital with proper identification and request official permission from the hospital administrator to speak with the patient

7. Among employment specialists, it is generally agreed that the value of character references on employment applications is

   A. *limited,* chiefly because such references are written only by personal friends of the applicant
   B. *significant,* chiefly because information they transmit is unavailable from other sources
   C. *limited,* chiefly because they tend to give only favorable information
   D. *significant,* chiefly because they have direct knowledge of the applicant's abilities

8. The MOST important requirement of a person who is testifying about a criminal act that he witnessed is that he

   A. was conscious and attentive during the crime
   B. is a respected and trustworthy member of the community
   C. is without a prior criminal record
   D. gives a consistent account of the details of the crime

9. Assume that, after taking a written statement from Employee A, an investigator is about to obtain his signature. He wants to ask Employee B, a co-worker, to witness the signing but Employee B is not available at that time.
   To expedite the investigation, it would be MOST desirable for the investigator to

   A. have Employee A sign the statement and obtain Employee B's signature at a later time
   B. ask an available disinterested party to witness Employee A's signature
   C. witness Employee A's signature himself
   D. have Employee A sign when Employee B is available

10. Witnesses are usually MOST willing to discuss an event when they are　10._____

    A. disinterested in the subsequent investigation
    B. interviewed immediately following the event
    C. interviewed for the first time
    D. known by the investigator

11. To determine the former addresses of a person who has moved several times within the same locality, it would be BEST to contact　11._____

    A. the Post Office   B. insurance companies
    C. public utilities   D. banking institutions

12. The one of the following that is CHARACTERISTIC of the interview as compared with the observation approach to investigation is that an interview generally　12._____

    A. requires more time to complete adequately
    B. is more likely to result in incomplete information
    C. is less applicable to the study of an individual's beliefs and values
    D. is less costly to conduct

13. The use of slang on the part of an investigator when questioning subjects is generally　13._____

    A. *inadvisable*; chiefly because it leads to misinterpretations
    B. *advisable*; chiefly because it will insure objective responses
    C. *inadvisable*; chiefly because it can compromise the investigator's dignity
    D. *advisable*; chiefly because it can promote ease of speech and understanding

14. Assume that a job applicant claims on his employment application that he has just recently become a United States citizen.
Of the following, it would be MOST appropriate for you, in verifying this matter, to consult the　14._____

    A. Department of State   B. Treasury Department
    C. Immigration and Naturalization Service D. Department of Justice

15. If an investigator receives an anonymous phone call from a person claiming to have knowledge of criminal behavior in an agency which is currently being investigated, the investigator should　15._____

    A. listen politely and make notes on the important facts given by the informant
    B. tell the informant what has already been discovered and ask if he has anything to add
    C. question the informant to obtain all the information he has
    D. ask the informant to submit his information in writing

16. When interviewing a child, an investigator should keep in mind the fact that children　16._____

    A. are psychologically incapable of giving an accurate statement
    B. usually have faulty perception
    C. are easily led into making incorrect statements since they tend to agree with the questioner
    D. will often make statements which are pure fantasy because they are not as observant as adults

17. Following are three statements concerning the use of an investigator's notebook in court:
    I. A looseleaf-type notebook creates a more favorable impression in the courtroom than a bound notebook because the former permits the removal of pages unrelated to the case in question
    II. An investigator's notebook should be written in ink, not pencil, because of the need for permanence
    III. The notebook should ideally contain the notes of only one investigation so that its scrutiny will not involve the disclosure of information relating to other investigations

    Which of the following CORRECTLY classifies the above statements into those which are valid and those which are not valid?

    A. I and III are valid, but II is not.
    B. I and II are valid, but III is not.
    C. I is valid, but II and III are not.
    D. II and III are valid, but I is not.

18. The first three digits of a social security number are coded for the

    A. age of the cardholder when the card was issued
    B. cardholder's initials
    C. year the card was issued
    D. area in which the card was issued

19. Two methods of obtaining personal background information are the personal interview and the telephone inquiry.
    As compared with the latter, the personal type of interview USUALLY _____ flexibility in questioning _____ frankness.

    A. permits; but discourages
    B. restricts; but encourages
    C. permits; and encourages
    D. restricts; and discourages

20. One of the important functions of investigators is to perform surveillances without the knowledge of the subject. If a subject thinks he is being followed, he is LEAST likely to react by

    A. reversing his course to see whether anyone else does likewise
    B. boarding a subway car and getting off just before it pulls out
    C. attempting to pass the surveillant several times to view him face-to-face
    D. using the services of a *convoy* to observe whether he is being followed

21. Assume that you are conducting an interview with a prospective employee who is of limited mental ability and low socio-economic status.
    Of the following, it is MOST likely that asking him many open-ended questions about his work experience would cause him to respond

    A. articulately
    B. reluctantly
    C. comfortably
    D. aggressively

22. Assume, as an investigator, you want a witness to sign a statement. Which of the following phrases is MOST likely to secure his signature?

    A. I would appreciate it if you would sign the statement at this time.
    B. Sign the statement where indicated.
    C. Sign the statement when you get the chance.
    D. If the statement is generally correct, please sign it.

23. During an interview, a subject makes statements an investigator knows to be false. Of the following, it would be MOST appropriate for the investigator to

    A. point out each inconsistency in the subject's story as soon as the investigator detects it
    B. interrupt the subject and request that he submit to a polygraph test
    C. allow the subject to continue talking until he becomes enmeshed in his lies and then confront him with his falsehoods
    D. allow the subject to finish what he has to say and then explicitly inform him that it is a crime to lie to a government employee

24. One of the major objectives of a pre-employment interview is to get the interviewee to respond freely to inquiries. The one of the following actions that would be MOST likely to restrict the conversation of the interviewee would be for the investigator to

    A. keep a stenographic record of the interviewee's statements
    B. ask questions requiring complete explanations
    C. pose direct, specific questions to the interviewee
    D. allow the interviewee to respond to questions at his own pace

25. A list of the names, addresses, and titles of city employees is made available to the public by the

    A. civil service commission
    B. comptroller's office
    C. mayor's office
    D. municipal reference and research center

KEY (CORRECT ANSWERS)

1.	D	11.	C
2.	A	12.	D
3.	A	13.	D
4.	B	14.	C
5.	A	15.	C
6.	B	16.	C
7.	C	17.	D
8.	A	18.	D
9.	B	19.	C
10.	B	20.	C

21. B
22. B
23. C
24. A
25. D

READING COMPREHENSION
UNDERSTANDING AND INTERPRETING WRITTEN MATERIAL
EXAMINATION SECTION
TEST 1

DIRECTIONS: Each question or incomplete statement is followed by several suggested answers or completions. Select the one that BEST answers the question or completes the statement. *PRINT THE LETTER OF THE CORRECT ANSWER IN THE SPACE AT THE RIGHT.*

Questions 1-4.

DIRECTIONS: Questions 1 through 4 are to be answered SOLELY on the basis of the information contained in the following passage.

After conducting and completing an interview, the interviewer is faced with the responsibility of recording it in some manner. Very considerable amounts of staff time and agency finances are absorbed in recording. Time and cost studies of agency expenditures indicate that, for every dollar spent on interviewing, three dollars are spent on recording. In addition to actual time spent by the worker in recording, such expense involves clerical transcribing time, filing time and space, and time in reading records.

Recording insures a continuity of client-agency contact that transcends the client's contact with any individual social worker. The case record also implements the agency's accountability to the community. It provides a permanent, documented account of services to clients. The interviewer about to record the interview faces the essential question, what should be recorded and how should the recording be organized? Just as purpose guides interview interaction, so it guides selection of material for recording. Traditionally, social work recording has been designed to meet a number of different purposes. We record to achieve more effective practice, to provide material for in-service training and teaching, and for research purposes. There is no consensus on the principal purpose of social work recording. Consequently, recording has served these various purposes with limited effectiveness, and has served no one purpose well.

1. According to the above passage, the relationship between recording and interviewing costs for social work purposes is such that

    A. recording is three times more expensive than interviewing
    B. recording is one-third as expensive as interviewing
    C. recording is four times more expensive than interviewing
    D. interviewing is much more expensive than recording

    1.____

2. The one of the following that is SPECIFICALLY mentioned as a purpose of case recording is

    A. saving time
    B. economy
    C. research
    D. convenience

    2.____

3. Of the following, according to the above passage, a MAJOR contributing factor to the expense of case recording is

   A. supervision
   B. in-service training
   C. research
   D. record reading time

4. It can be concluded that the author's opinion regarding the capacity of social work recording to achieve its various purposes is

   A. enthusiastic
   B. guarded
   C. neutral
   D. confused

Questions 5-7.

DIRECTIONS: Questions 5 through 7 are to be answered SOLELY on the basis of the information in the following passage.

It is important that interviewers understand to some degree the manner in which stereotyped thinking operates. Stereotypes are commonly held, but predominantly false, preoccupations about the appearance and traits of individuals of different racial, religious, ethnic, and subcultural groups. Distinct traits, physical and mental, are associated with each group, and membership in a particular group is enough, in the mind of a person holding the stereotype, to assure that these traits will be perceived in individuals who are members of that group. Conversely, possession of the particular stereotyped trait by an individual usually indicates to the holder of the stereotype that the individual is a group member. Linked to the formation of stereotypes is the fact that mental traits, either positive or negative, such as honesty, laziness, avariciousness, and other characteristics are associated with particular stereotypes. Either kind of stereotype, if held by an interviewer, can seriously damage the results of an interview. In general, stereotypes can be particularly dangerous when they are part of the belief patterns of administrators, interviewers, and supervisors, who are in a position to affect the lives of others and to stimulate or retard the development of human potential. The holding of a stereotype by an interviewer, for example, diverts his attention from significant essential facts and information upon which really valid assessments may be made. Unfortunately, it is the rare interviewer who is completely conscious of the real basis upon which he is making his evaluation of the people he is interviewing. The specific reasons given by an interviewer for a negative evaluation, even though apparently logical and based upon what, in the mind of the interviewer, are very good reasons, may not be the truly motivating factors. This is why the careful selection and training of interviewers is such an important responsibility of an agency which is attempting to help a great diversity of human beings.

5. Of the following, the BEST title for the above paragraph is

   A. POSITIVE AND NEGATIVE EFFECTS OF STEREOTYPED THINKING
   B. THE RELATIONSHIP OF STEREOTYPES TO INTERVIEWING
   C. AN AGENCY'S RESPONSIBILITY IN INTERVIEWING
   D. THE IMPACT OF STEREOTYPED THINKING ON PROFESSIONAL FUNCTIONS

6. According to the above passage, MOST interviewers

   A. compensate for stereotyped beliefs to avoid negatively affecting the results of their interviews
   B. are influenced by stereotypes they hold, but put greater stress on factual information developed during the interview
   C. are seldom aware of their real motives when evaluating interviewees
   D. give logical and good reasons for negative evaluations of interviewees

7. According to the above passage, which of the following is NOT a characteristic of stereotypes?

   A. Stereotypes influence estimates of personality traits of people.
   B. Positive stereotypes can damage the results of an interview.
   C. Physical traits associated with stereotypes seldom really exist.
   D. Stereotypes sometimes are a basis upon which valid personality assessments can be made.

Questions 8-12.

DIRECTIONS: Questions 8 through 12 are to be answered SOLELY on the basis of the following passage.

At one time, people thought that in the interview designed primarily to obtain information, the interviewer had to resort to clever and subtle lines of questioning in order to accomplish his ends. Some people still believe that this is necessary, but it is not so. An example of the *tricky* approach may be seen in the work of a recent study. The study deals with materials likely to be buried beneath deep defenses. Interviewers utilized methods of questioning which, in effect, trapped the interviewee and destroyed his defenses. Doubtless, these methods succeeded in bringing out items of information which straightforward questions would have missed. Whether they missed more information than they obtained and whether they obtained the most important facts must remain unanswered questions. In defense of the *clever* approach, it is often said that, in many situations, the interviewee is motivated to conceal information or to distort what he chooses to report.

Technically, it is likely that a highly skilled interviewer can, given the time and the inclination, penetrate the interviewee's defenses and get information which the latter intended to keep hidden. It is unlikely that the interviewer can successfully elicit all of the information that might be relevant. If, for example, he found that an applicant for financial assistance was heavily in debt to gamblers, he might not care about getting any other information. There are situations in which one item, if answered in the *wrong* way, is enough. Ordinarily, this is not true. The usual situation is that there are many considerations and that the plus and minus features must be weighed before a decision may be made. It is, therefore, important to obtain complete information.

8. According to the above passage, it was GENERALLY believed that an interviewer would have difficulty in obtaining the information he sought from a person if he

   A. were tricky in his methods
   B. were open and frank in his approach

C. were clever in his questioning
D. utilized carefully prepared questions

9. The passage does NOT reveal whether the type of questions used

   A. trapped those being interviewed
   B. elicited facts which an open method of questioning might miss
   C. elicited the most important facts that were sought
   D. covered matters which those interviewed were reluctant to talk about openly

10. An argument in favor of the *tricky* or *clever* interviewing technique is that, unless this approach is used, the person interviewed will NOT

    A. offer to furnish all pertinent information
    B. answer questions concerning routine data
    C. clearly understand what is being sought
    D. want to continue the interview

11. According to the above passage, in favorable circumstances, a talented interviewer would be able to obtain from the person interviewed information

    A. which the person regards as irrelevant
    B. which the person intends to conceal
    C. about the person's family background
    D. which the person would normally have forgotten

12. According to the above passage, a highly skilled interviewer should concentrate, in most cases, on getting

    A. one outstanding fact about the interviewee which would do away with the need for prolonged questioning
    B. facts which the interviewee wanted to conceal because these would be the most relevant in making a decision
    C. all the facts so that he can consider their relative values before reaching any conclusion
    D. information about any bad habits of the interviewee, such as gambling, which would make further questioning

Questions 13-14.

DIRECTIONS: Questions 13 and 14 are to be answered SOLELY on the basis of the information given below.

The ability to interview rests not on any single trait, but on a vast complex of them. Habits, skills, techniques, and attitudes are all involved. Competence in interviewing is acquired only after careful and diligent study, prolonged practice (preferably under supervision), and a good bit of trial and error; for interviewing is not an exact science, it is an art. Like many other arts, however, it can and must draw on science in several of its aspects.

There is always a place for individual initiative, for imaginative innovations, and for new combinations of old approaches. The skilled interviewer cannot be bound by a set of rules. Likewise, there is not a set of rules which can guarantee to the novice that his interviewing will be successful. There are, however, some accepted, general guideposts which may help the beginner to avoid mistakes, learn how to conserve his efforts, and establish effective working relationships with interviewees; to accomplish, in short, what he sets out to do.

13. According to the above passage, rules and standard techniques for interviewing are

    A. helpful for the beginner, but useless for the experienced, innovative interviewer
    B. destructive of the innovation and initiative needed for a good interviewer
    C. useful for even the experienced interviewer who may, however, sometimes go beyond them
    D. the means by which nearly anybody can become an effective interviewer

14. According to the above passage, the one of the following which is a prerequisite to competent interviewing is

    A. avoiding mistakes
    B. study and practice
    C. imaginative innovation
    D. natural aptitude

Questions 15-17.

DIRECTIONS: Questions 15 through 17 are to be answered SOLELY on the basis of the following paragraph.

The physical setting of the interview may determine its entire potentiality. Some degree of privacy and a comfortable relaxed atmosphere are important. The interviewee is not encouraged to give much more than his name and address if the interviewer seems busy with other things, if people are rushing about, if there are distracting noises. He has a right to feel that, whether the interview lasts five minutes or an hour, he has, for that time, the undivided attention of the interviewer. If the interviewee has waited in a crowded room for what seems to him an interminably long period, he is naturally in no mood to sit down and discuss what is on his mind. Indeed, by that time the primary thing on his mind may be his irritation at being kept waiting, and he frequently feels it would be impolite to express this. If a wait or interruptions have been unavoidable, it is always helpful to give the client some recognition that these are disturbing and that we can naturally understand that they make it more difficult for him to proceed. At the same time, if he protests that they have not troubled him, the interviewer can best accept his statements at their face value, as further insistence that they must have been disturbing may be interpreted by his as accusing, and he may conclude that the interviewer has been personally hurt by his irritation.

15. Distraction during an interview may tend to limit the client's responses.
    In a case where an interruption has occurred, it would be BEST for the investigator to

    A. terminate this interview and have it rescheduled for another time period
    B. ignore the interruption since it is not continuous
    C. express his understanding that the distraction can cause the client to feel disturbed
    D. accept the client's protests that he has been troubled by the interruption

16. To maximize the rapport that can be established with the client, an appropriate physical setting is necessary. At the very least, some privacy would be necessary.
In addition, the interviewer should

    A. always appear to be busy in order to impress the client
    B. focus his attention only on the client
    C. accept all the client's statements as being valid
    D. stress the importance of the interview to the client

17. Clients who have been waiting quite some time for their interview may, justifiably, become upset.
However, a client may INITIALLY attempt to mask these feelings because he may

    A. personally hurt the interviewer
    B. want to be civil
    C. feel that the wait was unavoidable
    D. fear the consequences of his statement

Questions 18-20.

DIRECTIONS: Questions 18 through 20 are to be answered SOLELY on the basis of information given in the passage below.

A personnel interviewer, selecting job applicants, may find that he reacts badly to some people even on first contact. This reaction cannot usually be explained by things that the interviewee has done or said. Most of us have had the experience of liking or disliking, of feeling comfortable or uncomfortable with people on first acquaintance, long before we have had a chance to make a conscious, rational decision about them. Often, too, our liking or disliking is transmitted to the other person by subtle processes such as gestures, posture, voice intonations, or choice of words. The point to be kept in mind is this: the relations between people are complex and occur at several levels, from the conscious to the unconscious. This is true whether the relationship is brief or long, formal or informal.

Some of the major dynamics of personality which operate on the unconscious level are projection, sublimation, rationalization, and repression. Encountering these for the first time, one is apt to think of them as representing pathological states. In the extreme, they undoubtedly are, but they exist so universally that we must consider them also to be parts of normal personality.

Without necessarily subscribing to any of the numerous theories of personality, it is possible to describe personality in terms of certain important aspects or elements. We are all aware of ourselves as thinking organisms.

This aspect of personality, the conscious part, is important for understanding human behavior, but it is not enough. Many find it hard to accept the notion that each person also has an unconscious. The existence of the unconscious is no longer a matter of debate. It is not possible to estimate at all precisely what proportion of our total psychological life is conscious, what proportion unconscious. Everyone who has studied the problem, however, agrees that consciousness is the smaller part of personality. Most of what we are and do is a result of unconscious processes. To ignore this is to risk mistakes.

18. The above passage suggests that an interviewer can be MOST effective if he

    A. learns how to determine other peoples' unconscious motivations
    B. learns how to repress his own unconsciously motivated mannerisms and behavior
    C. can keep others from feeling that he either likes or dislikes them
    D. gains an understanding of how the unconscious operates in himself and in others

19. It may be inferred from the above passage that the *subtle processes such as gestures, posture, voice intonation, or choice of words* referred to in the first paragraph are USUALLY

    A. in the complete control of an expert investigator
    B. the determining factors in the friendships a person establishes
    C. controlled by a person's unconscious
    D. not capable of being consciously controlled

20. The above passage implies that various different personality theories are USUALLY

    A. so numerous and different as to be valueless to an investigator
    B. in basic agreement about the importance of the unconscious
    C. understood by the investigator who strives to be effective
    D. in agreement that personality factors such as projection and repression are pathological

Questions 21-25.

DIRECTIONS: Questions 21 through 25 are to be answered SOLELY on the basis of the information given in the following paragraph.

The nature of the interview varies with the aim or the use to which it is put. While these uses vary widely, interviews are basically of three types: fact-finding, informing, and motivating. One of these purposes usually predominates in an interview, but not to the exclusion of the other two. If the main purpose is fact-finding, for example, the interviewer must often motivate the interviewee to cooperate in revealing the facts. A major factor in the interview is the interaction of the personalities of the interviewer and the interviewee. The interviewee may not wish to reveal the facts sought, or even though willing enough to impart them, he may not be able to do so because of a lack of clear understanding as to what is wanted or because of lack of ability to put into words the information he has to give. On the other hand, the interviewer may not be able to grasp and report accurately the facts which the one being interviewed is trying to convey. Also, the interviewer's prejudice may make him not want to get at the real facts or make him unable to recognize the truth.

21. According to the above paragraph, the purpose of an interview

    A. determines the nature of the interview
    B. is usually the same for the three basic types of interviews
    C. is predominantly motivation of the interviewee
    D. is usually to check on the accuracy of facts previously obtained

22. In discussing the use or purpose of an interview, the above paragraph points out that
    A. a good interview should have only one purpose
    B. an interview usually has several uses that are equally important
    C. fact-finding should be the main purpose of an interview
    D. the interview usually has one main purpose

23. According to the above paragraph, an obstacle to the successful interview sometimes attributable to the interviewee is
    A. a lack of understanding of how to conduct an interview
    B. an inability to express himself
    C. prejudice toward the interviewer
    D. too great a desire to please

24. According to the above paragraph, one way in which the interviewer may help the interviewee to reveal the facts sought is to
    A. make him willing to impart the facts by stating clearly the consequences of false information
    B. make sure he understands what information is wanted
    C. motivate him by telling him how important he is in the investigation
    D. tell him what words to use to convey the information wanted

25. According to the above paragraph, bias on the part of the interviewer could
    A. be due to inability to understand the facts being imparted
    B. lead him to report the facts accurately
    C. make the interviewee unwilling to impart the truth
    D. prevent him from determining the facts

KEY (CORRECT ANSWERS)

1.	A	11.	B
2.	C	12.	C
3.	D	13.	C
4.	B	14.	B
5.	B	15.	C
6.	C	16.	B
7.	D	17.	B
8.	B	18.	D
9.	C	19.	C
10.	A	20.	B

21. A
22. D
23. B
24. B
25. D

Glossary of Legal Investigative Terms

A

ABANDONMENT - Desertion by a husband or wife of his or her spouse with the intention of creating a permanent separation.

ABSCOND - To hide from the jurisdiction of a court in order to avoid a legal process.

ACCESSORY AFTER THE FACT - A person who, after the commission of a felony, conceals the offender with the intent that the latter may escape from arrest.

ACCESSORY BEFORE THE FACT - A person who aids and abets in the planning of the commission of a crime, although he may not participate in the actual commission of the crime.

ACCOMPLICE - A person who is liable to prosecution for the identical offense charged against a defendant on trial.

ACQUIT - To free a person legally from an accusation of criminal guilt.

AFFIDAVIT - A written statement under oath.

ALIBI - Evidence showing that a defendant was in another place when the crime was committed.

APPEAL - A review by higher court to determine whether the decision or verdict in the lower court should be reversed, modified, or affirmed.

ARBITRATION - The settlement of a disagreement out of court by an arbitrator chosen by the parties to the argument.

ARRAIGNMENT - Calling a defendant before the court to answer an accusation.

ARSON - The willful and malicious burning of property.

ASSAULT - An unlawful attempt to hurt another person physically or to place him in fear of being hurt physically.

ATTACHMENT - The legal seizure of the property of a defendant before judgment.

AUTOPSY - The dissection of a dead human body by an authorized doctor to determine the cause of death.

B

BAIL - To set free or liberate from arrest and imprisonment, upon security given that the person released shall appear and answer in court. (See Jump Bail)

BALLISTICS - The examination of bullets that have been fired for the purpose of discovering from which weapon a given bullet has been fired. The science that deals with the motion of projectiles.

BARRATRY - Inciting groundless judicial proceedings.

BENCH WARRANT - A court order directing that an offender be brought into court.

BLACKMAIL - The extortion of goods, money or the procuring of an illegal act by a threat, in writing, of criminal prosecution or the destruction of a person's reputation or social standing or personal injury.

BRIBERY - Promising or offering money to a witness or an executive officer to influence his action or testimony.

BUG - A device concealed on a subject's premises for the purpose of listening to conversations taking place.

BURGLARY - Breaking and entering a building with intent to commit some crime therein.

C

CAPITAL OFFENSE - A crime for which a life sentence or the death penalty is prescribed by law.

CAPTAIN - A term used to describe a supervisor of professional strike breakers.

CHAMPERTY - An agreement whereby a stranger to a suit agrees to finance one side in return for a share of the property that is secured through the action.

CIRCUMSTANTIAL EVIDENCE - Evidence which includes facts, conditions, and events from which an inference may be drawn as to the existence of the fact to be established.

CONFESSION - A statement by a person accused of a crime admitting his guilt.

CONSPIRACY - A combination of two or more persons to accomplish a criminal or unlawful act.

CONTEMPT OF COURT - Behavior disrespectful of the authority of a court which obstructs the execution of court orders.

CONTRACT - An agreement to do or not to do a certain thing which is enforceable in court.

CORPUS DELICTI - The actual visible proof that a crime has been committed. In homicide cases, the term used to designate the victim.

CORROBORATIVE EVIDENCE - Strengthening or confirming evidence given in support of the truth of facts testified by another witness.

COURT OF EQUITY - A court which administers justice according to the principles of equity. (See Equity)

D

DEMUR - Raise an objection in point of law, referring the decision thereon to the court.

DEMURRER - In court procedure, a statement that the opposing party has no sufficient basis in law despite the truth of the facts advanced.

DEPOSITION - A sworn statement made before an officer qualified to administer oaths, which is to be used as evidence in a court proceeding.

DIRECT EVIDENCE - The statement of a witness who has actual knowledge of the facts to be proved because he saw or otherwise observed with his senses the commission of the act.

DISORDERLY CONDUCT - A minor offense which tends to endanger public peace, safety, or morals.

DURESS - To force a person against his will to perform or refrain from performing an act.

E

EMBEZZLEMENT - Fraudulent appropriation by a person acting in a fiduciary capacity of money or property entrusted by another.

EMBRACERY - The attempt to corruptly influence a juror.

ENTRAPMENT - To induce one to commit a crime not contemplated by him for the purpose of investigating a prosecution against him.

EQUITY - That branch of the law which endeavors to do justice in those situations where the ordinary court of law affords no remedy. (See Court of Equity)

ESTOPPEL - A legal prohibition which stops a person from making a particular statement or claim because of something he has said or done before.

EXECUTOR - The person named by a tester to carry out the provisions of his will.

EX PARTE - Something which is done by or for one side only and without notice to any person adversely interested.

EXTORTION - Taking or obtaining property from another with his consent, induced by a wrongful use of force or fear.

EXTRADITION - Delivery from one state or nation to another, of fugitives from justice.

F

FELONY - A crime punishable by death or imprisonment in a state prison.

FIDUCIARY - Having the character of a trustee; invested with rights and powers to be exercised with an obligation of loyalty for the benefit of some other person.

FINK - A professional strike breaker.

FORGERY - The falsely making or materially altering, with intent to defraud, any writing which, if genuine, might apparently be of some legal effect upon the rights of others.

G

GARNISHMENT - The attachment of a debtor's wages or salary to satisfy or pay a judgment.

GENERAL RELEASE - A formal document made out by an individual certifying that he has no further cause of action against another.

GRAND JURY - An official body, consisting of a group of 23 citizens, called to hear complaints of a criminal nature and to determine whether there is ground for legal prosecution.

GRAND LARCENY - Unlawfully taking property belonging to another, which is valued at more than $100.

H

HABEAS CORPUS - A written order commanding the bringing of the body of a certain person before a certain court.

HEARSAY EVIDENCE - Testimony by one person that another person had told him about a criminal action which the other person had witnessed. (Generally inadmissible)

HOMICIDE - Killing of one human being by the act or omission of another human being.

I

INDICTMENT - The accusation in writing presented by the Grand Jury to a competent court charging a person with a crime.

INJUNCTION - A writ or order issued by a court or judge requiring a person to refrain from a particular act.

INQUEST - A public hearing to determine the cause of death of a human being.

INTESTATE - A person who dies without having a valid will or testament. IPSO FACTO - By the mere effect of an act or a fact.

J

JOSTLING - Unnecessarily crowding against a person or placing a hand in the proximity of such person's pocket, pocketbook, or han'dbag.

JUDGMENT - The official decision of a court or justice on the claims of parties to a litigation.

JUMP BAIL .- Failure to make an appearance in court in accordance with the terms imposed at the time bail is fixed. (See Bail)

JURAT - That part of an affidavit where the officer certifies that it was sworn to before him.

K

KLEPTOMANIAC - A person who has a strong desire to shoplift or to steal even though he has plenty of money to pay for the things stolen.

L

LACHES - Failure to assert a right for an unreasonable length of time. (Generally creates an estoppel)

LARCENY - Unlawfully taking property belonging to another.

LEVY - Taking possession of property by an official to satisfy a judgment.

LIBEL - Writing calculated to injure the reputation of another by bringing him to ridicule, hatred, or contempt.

LIBEL (ADMIRALTY LAW) - A written statement made by the plaintiff of his cause of action and of the relief that he seeks*

LIEN - A legal right or claim upon a specific property which holds the property until a debt is satisfied.

LIS PENDENS - A legal document filed in the office of the county clerk giving notice that an action or proceeding is pending in the courts affecting the title to real property.

M

MALINGERING - The act of feigning or faking an illness or injury.

MANDAMUS - An instrument in writing ordering a court or administrative officer to perform some specific duty.

MANSLAUGHTER - The unlawful killing of another without malice either express or implied.

MAYHEM - The act of wilfully depriving another of the use of one or more of his limbs so that he is less capable of defending himself.

MISDEMEANOR - A crime which is not punishable by imprisonment in a state prison or death. (See Felony)

MODUS OPERANDI - The term used to indicate the method or technique followed in the performance of a criminal act.

MORAL TURPITUDE - The quality of a crime involving grave infringement of the moral sentiment of the community (as distinguished from the statutory). (See Turpitude)

N

NEGLIGENCE ACTIONS - The general class of civil suits arising from the defendant's failure to exercise reasonable care.

O

OBITER DICTUM - A remark made by a judge in his decision which does not bear directly upon the question before him.

ORDINANCE - A law passed by a local authority.

P

PAROLE - A conditional release from prison.

PEREMPTORY CHALLENGE - The right of the prisoner and the prosecution, in a criminal trial to offer objection to a certain number of jurors without giving any explanation.

PERJURY - The act of wilfully swearing falsely.

PETIT JURY - The ordinary jury of men or women for the trial of a civil or criminal action.

PETIT LARCENY - Unlawfully taking property belonging to another which is valued at less than $100.

PHYSICAL EVIDENCE - Anything that may be found by expert investigators to have a connection with a crime (for example, an article of clothing worn by the victim).

S

SENTENCE - A judgment passed by a court on a person on trial as a criminal offender.

SHADOWING - An observed close watch.

SLANDER - A verbal statement calculated to injure the reputation of another by bringing him into ridicule, hatred, or contempt.

SPOTTING - Making known the identity of an undercover operator. (A term also used) To point out or identify a subject to be shadowed.

STATUTE OF LIMITATIONS - A law which limits the time within which a criminal prosecution or a civil action must be started.

SUBPOENA - A writ or order directed to a person and requiring his attendance at a particular time and place to testify as a witness.

SUBPOENA DUCES TECUM - A subpoena not only requiring the witness to testify, but also to compel him to bring all books, documents, and papers that may have any bearing on the outcome of the proceedings.

SUBORNATION OF PERJURY - Wilfully procuring or inducing another to testify falsely under oath.

SUBROGATION - Substitution of one person's claims, rights, or securities for those of another person.

SUI JURIS - Being fully able to manage one's own affairs.

SUMMARY PROCEEDINGS - A form of trial before a judge without a jury and without following the rules of procedure applicable to trials.

SUMMONS - A writ commanding the sheriff or other authorized person to notify a party to appear in court to answer a complaint made against him and in the said writ specified, on a day therein mentioned.

<u>T</u>

TESTATOR - A person who makes a last will and testament.

TESTIMONY - Any statement or statements made by witnesses under oath in a judicial proceeding.

TORT - A legal wrong committed against a person or property for which reparation may be obtained by a suit at law.

TRESPASS - Entering any real property or structure of any kind without consent.

TRUE BILL - An indictment handed down by a Grand Jury.

TURPITUDE - Everything done contrary to justice, honesty, modesty, or good morals is said to be done with turpitude.

<u>U</u>

UNLAWFUL ENTRY - Entering a building, without breaking, with intent to commit some crime therein.

V

VENUE - The neighborhood, place, or county in which an injury is declared to have been done, or fact declared to have happened.

W

WARRANT - A writ issued by a court authorizing the arrest of a person, or the seizure of property.

WRIT - Any directive to a court or administrative officer.

www.ingramcontent.com/pod-product-compliance
Lightning Source LLC
Chambersburg PA
CBHW082209300426
44117CB00016B/2737